POWer Words™

Grades 7–8

Activities to develop student vocabulary and expand word power

by
M. B. Zappala

Printed in the U.S.A.

Author: M. B. Zappala   **Editor:** Heather M. Marnan   **Page Layout & Graphics:** Adrienne M. Speer

These popular teacher resources and activity books are available from
ECS Learning Systems, Inc.

ECS2371	Grammar Notebook: Parts of Speech	Grades 9–12
ECS238X	Grammar Notebook: Sentence Structure	Grades 9–12
ECS2398	Grammar Notebook: Punctuation, Capitalization, and Spelling	Grades 9–12
NU783XRH	Graphic Organizer Collection	Grades 3–12
ECS0484	Not More Writing?!	Grades 9–12
ECS9706	Springboards for Reading	Grades 7–12
NU5958RH	Tackling Literary Terms	Grades 9–12
ECS9463	Writing Warm-Ups Two	Grades 7–12
ECS8414	POWer Words™	Grades 5–6
ECS5494	POWer Words™	Grades 9–12
ECS6564	POWer Strategies™ for Reading Comprehension	Grades 3–5
ECS6571	POWer Strategies™ for Reading Comprehension	Grades 6–8

To order, or for a complete catalog, write:
ECS Learning Systems, Inc., P.O. Box 440, Bulverde, TX 78163-0440
Web site: **ecslearningsystems.com**
1 • 800 • 688 • 3224

ISBN 978-1-57022-521-5

POWer Words™

Grades 7–8

by
M. B. Zappala

Table of Contents

About the Author

M. B. Zappala is an educational consultant and reading/language arts specialist with 25 years of teaching experience. She received her B.A. in history from Rivier College in Nashua, New Hampshire. She was awarded her M.S. in education from Hofstra University in Hempstead, New York, where she also completed post-graduate work in reading and administration.

Mrs. Zappala has trained teachers, taught language arts courses, and presented numerous papers and workshops at International Reading Association conferences. She has also presented workshops for high school students and their parents designed to facilitate the college application experience. These workshops include, "From An Ordinary Day—A Winning Essay," "Making the Most of the College Tour and Interview," and "How to Prepare for College and Maintain Peace in the Home."

Introduction

Purpose

POWer Words™ is a comprehensive review of 500 difficult vocabulary words found on most standardized tests. Students might recognize many of the words presented in *POWer Words*™, but they may not know the correct uses of the words. *POWer Words*™ offers a thorough study of vocabulary by helping students to:

- develop a broader knowledge of words and their meanings
- recognize relationships between different groups of words
- apply complex vocabulary to everyday situations
- attain a more elaborate method of speaking and writing

Unlike most traditional vocabulary textbooks, *POWer Words*™ provides students with an interesting and non-repetitive study of semantics and word usage.

Format

POWer Words™ is organized into 20 Vocabulary Lists. Each list contains words that support a common theme (e.g., school, people, money). Three practice activities follow each Vocabulary List and are supported by review activities throughout the book. The practice and review activities utilize a variety of formats, such as multiple-choice items, fill in the blanks, and crossword puzzles. An Index is included on pp. 127–131 of this book. The Index provides the Vocabulary List in which each word appears, allowing for quick reference of a particular word.

Student Response/Answer Key

Many of the activities in *POWer Words*™ lend themselves to several correct answers, particularly the Sentence Completion and Passage Completion activities. In such cases, the Answer Key provides one set of possible answers; however, there may be other correct answers. For example, on a Passage Completion activity in which a word box is not provided, the student could complete the passage many different ways. The student's word choices will affect the meaning and feeling portrayed in the passage, and although they may differ from the Answer Key, they are not necessarily incorrect. Remember that the Answer Key offers only one set of possible answers for such activities. Encourage students to discuss their answers and give valid justification for their choices.

Notes

It's your first day in a new school.

As you walk through the door you are...

flustered (adj.) made nervous and unsure; upset; disturbed
inhibited (adj.) finding it hard to show feelings; reserved; self-conscious
perplexed (adj.) confused; bewildered; puzzled
susceptible (adj.) easily influenced; vulnerable
tremulous (adj.) fearful; timid; trembling; shaky

Everyone else seems so...

boisterous (adj.) noisy and lively; loud and exuberant; rowdy
genial (adj.) cordial; friendly; sociable; affable
motivated (adj.) persuaded to do something; inspired; influenced
oblivious (adj.) unaware of; unconcerned; inattentive
peculiar (adj.) different from the usual; odd; eccentric; unique
spontaneous (adj.) unprompted; unplanned; acting without thought

Relax—before long you will...

accommodate (v.) adapt; adjust; help; have the capacity for
anticipate (v.) look forward to; count on; await
assert (v.) state clearly and strongly with confidence; declare
assimilate (v.) blend in; take something in and make it a part of you
prove your **mettle** (n.) spirit; determination; fortitude; nerve; grit
mingle (v.) associate; join; blend; fuse
transcend (v.) rise above; exceed; surpass; outshine

Soon you too will become...

buoyant (adj.) enthusiastic; cheerful; optimistic; capable of floating
competent (adj.) capable; qualified
dogged (adj.) persistent; stubbornly determined; refusing to give up
elated (adj.) filled with joy and pride; in high spirits; excited
eloquent (adj.) convincing; persuasive; stirring
jovial (adj.) full of good humor; cheerful; friendly
keen (adj.) full of enthusiasm; alert; clever; having a sharp edge

Choose the correct word from Vocabulary List 1 for each item.

_____ 1. adapt

    a. genial

    b. mettle

    c. accommodate

_____ 2. unique

    a. peculiar

    b. tremulous

    c. buoyant

_____ 3. inspired to do something

    a. genial

    b. motivated

    c. perplexed

_____ 4. join

    a. mingle

    b. perplexed

    c. competent

_____ 5. made nervous and unsure

    a. susceptible

    b. flustered

    c. competent

_____ 6. friendly

    a. inhibited

    b. dogged

    c. genial

_____ 7. unaware of

    a. oblivious

    b. anticipate

    c. keen

_____ 8. adapt; fit in

    a. keen

    b. jovial

    c. assimilate

_____ 9. confused

    a. transcend

    b. perplexed

    c. boisterous

_____ 10. look forward to

    a. anticipate

    b. assert

    c. inhibited

_____ 11. state clearly

    a. jovial

    b. assert

    c. flustered

_____ 12. easily influenced

    a. susceptible

    b. dogged

    c. elated

_____ 13. reserved; self-conscious

    a. mettle

    b. inhibited

    c. elated

_____ 14. noisy and lively

    a. elevated

    b. buoyant

    c. boisterous

_____ 15. fearful

    a. tremulous

    b. mingle

    c. oblivious

_____ 16. unprompted

    a. assimilate

    b. spontaneous

    c. transcend

Match the definition in Column 1 to the correct word from Vocabulary List 1 in Column 2.

Column 1   **Column 2**

_____ 1. filled with joy; excited   a. assert

_____ 2. adapt; adjust   b. dogged

_____ 3. nervous; upset   c. elated

_____ 4. rise above   d. flustered

_____ 5. unaware of   e. tremulous

_____ 6. fit in   f. keen

_____ 7. easily influenced   g. assimilate

_____ 8. confused; bewildered   h. transcend

_____ 9. capable of floating   i. buoyant

_____10. timid; fearful; shaky   j. anticipate

_____11. spirit; nerve   k. oblivious

_____12. persuasive; convincing   l. susceptible

_____13. capable   m. jovial

_____14. alert and clever   n. accommodate

_____15. unplanned   o. eloquent

_____16. refusing to give up   p. perplexed

_____17. look forward to   q. spontaneous

_____18. socialize   r. competent

_____19. full of good humor   s. mingle

_____20. state clearly   t. mettle

Complete the passage below using words from Vocabulary List 1.

A Happy Meal

Katelyn stood outside her brother's car, balancing a tray of cheeseburgers, french fries, ice cream, and drinks in one hand while reaching for the door handle with the other. She was quite (1)_____. Her brother sat in the car, eyes closed and (2)_____ to her need for help. Katelyn had *never* been able to (3)_____ her brother's reaction to *any* situation at *any* time. While he was normally a very (4)_____ and considerate person, there were times that she could not easily (5)_____ herself to his (6)_____ behavior. Ten minutes before, he had been (7)_____ enough to describe exactly what to order and how much it would cost—to the penny! Now, with his favorite food just inches from his hands, he didn't seem interested or (8)_____ enough to open the door and give her a hand. Frustrated and a bit angry, she pressed her face against his window and cried out several times in a(n) (9)_____ and pitiful voice, "Brian, please open the d-o-o-o-r!" Her (10)_____ attempts to attract his attention were in vain, but instead drew a(n) (11)_____ crowd of curious passersby who loudly cheered her efforts. Their (12)_____ comments and jests proved to be a more (13)_____ message than Katelyn's pleas. Brian looked up, noticed the tray of food, and rolled down the window. With a big grin on his face, he asked, "Hey, Sis! What's up? Need a hand with that? Boy, am I ever starved! What's been keeping you?" (14)_____ cheers and laughter rang out from the watching crowd.

Katelyn was not usually (15)_____ to temper tantrums or angry outbursts. While she often appeared (16)_____ in reacting to uncomfortable or embarrassing situations, she had always had the (17)_____ to get through without losing her positive, (18)_____ attitude towards life. But now she failed to (19)_____ the laughter of the unwanted spectators and her brother's behavior, and a darker force began to (20)_____ control. Try as she might, she did not have the strength to (21)_____ the desire to express how she felt. She gently tipped the tray downwards towards her brother, allowing burgers, fries, and ice cream to (22)_____ like the best of friends and slide together off the tray. His (23)_____ grin turned to a look of pure horror as lunch, and perhaps justice, was served.

Become the "Great Brainiac"

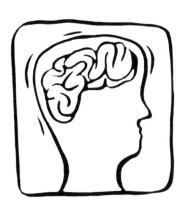

Develop curiosity

be **inquisitive** (adj.) eager for knowledge; curious; prying
perceive (v.) understand; grasp; become aware of; observe
ponder (v.) consider carefully; reflect on; think over
query (v.) ask questions of; investigate; challenge
be **rational** (adj.) sensible; reasonable; logical; clearheaded
reflect (v.) think seriously and carefully; consider; reveal; uncover
speculate (v.) wonder about a subject; wager; gamble

Energize!

collaborate (v.) work together; team up; cooperate; assist
cope (v.) try to manage; deal with something successfully; handle
cram (v.) study hard before a test; stuff; fill to overflowing
grapple (v.) attempt to deal with; face; come to grips with
persevere (v.) keep at something in spite of difficulties; refuse to quit
be **persistent** (adj.) stubbornly determined; constant; lasting
yearn (v.) want; crave; have a strong desire for; pine for

Get real—avoid the unclear and boring

cliché (n.) overused expression; stereotype
garbled (adj.) confused; distorted in such a way as to make unintelligible
humdrum (adj.) routine; mundane; tedious; unvarying
illegible (adj.) impossible or very hard to read; scribbled
illiterate (adj.) badly written; unable to read or write; uninstructed
incoherent (adj.) not clear or understandable in speech or thought
incomprehensible (adj.) impossible to understand; baffling; abstruse
indefinite (adj.) vague; not certain; not clear in meaning
irrelevant (adj.) not applicable or pertinent; unconnected
monotonous (adj.) boring; uninteresting; uttered in an unchanging tone
rambling (v.) talking or writing without a clear purpose or point; wandering

Solve the crossword puzzle below using words from Vocabulary List 2.

Across

6. work together
9. have a strong desire for
10. try to manage
12. confused
13. think seriously and carefully
14. curious
15. stubbornly determined

Down

1. wonder about a subject
2. come to grips with
3. ask questions of
4. very hard to read
5. refuse to quit
6. study hard for a test
7. sensible
8. consider carefully
11. understand

Complete each sentence with the correct word from the box below.

perceived	cram	humdrum	garbled	monotonous
ramble	illegible	cliché	illiterate	incomprehensible
grapple	inquisitive	irrelevant	indefinite	pondered
rational				

1. Static made it difficult to understand the _____ message left on my cell phone.

2. Memorizing history facts may seem _____ but helpful when preparing for a test.

3. The candidate's _____-ridden speech made little impact on the audience.

4. What your friends do is totally _____ when your parents establish their house rules.

5. If your handwriting is _____ it would be better to type your report.

6. Those _____ everyday drills that athletes perform help to create a winning team.

7. Our class collected books to aid the _____ members of the community.

8. He _____ a grave problem; would it be plain or pepperoni pizza?

9. It is _____ that some students go to class each day unprepared.

10. You will be grounded for a(n) _____ period if you come home after curfew.

11. One must make an effort to present a(n) _____ oral report instead of one that may _____ on and on.

12. Some friends become upset at any _____ slight; even an unreturned call becomes an insult.

13. Will I always have to _____ with the mysteries of math?

14. Have you ever wondered how they _____ all those clowns in a mini car at the circus?

15. A concerned neighbor is a gift, but an overly _____ one is just plain nosey.

Use words from Vocabulary List 2 to find the hidden message.

"What happened to the camper caught in a thunderstorm as he cooked outside his tent?"

1. __ Ⓞ __ __ __ Ⓞ   overused expression

2. __ __ __ Ⓞ   try to manage

3. __ __ __ Ⓞ __ __ __   routine; unvarying

4. __ __ __ Ⓞ __ __ __ Ⓞ __   wonder about something

5. Ⓞ __ __ __ __ __ Ⓞ __ __ __   unclear in speech

6. __ __ Ⓞ __ __ __ __   think seriously about

7. Ⓞ __ __ __ __ Ⓞ __ __   wander

8. __ __ Ⓞ __ __ __   investigate

Hidden Message: "He was __ __ __ __ __ __ __ - __ __ __ __ __."
                              2 1 8 4 4 7 5   6 5 7 1 3

How to ace that science class

Think like a scientist

analyze (v.) study something carefully; investigate
make a **conjecture** (n.) conclusion based on guess work; inference
evolve (v.) develop gradually; expand; change for the better
make a **hypothesis** (n.) a prediction that can be tested; assumption; proposal
predict (v.) guess in advance; anticipate; foretell; prognosticate
verify (v.) confirm; establish the truth of

Speak like a scientist

arid (adj.) not having enough rain; extremely dry; dull; uninteresting
inert (adj.) motionless; inactive; listless; torpid
palpable (adj.) obvious; noticeable; certain; able to be felt
porous (adj.) full of tiny holes; capable of absorbing liquids; absorbent
tepid (adj.) neither hot nor cold; lukewarm; half-hearted; indifferent
toxic (adj.) poisonous; lethal; causing harm

Tune in to the Science Fair chatter

astronomy (n.) the science of stars, planets, and space
celestial (adj.) having to do with the stars, planets, or sky; blissful; ethereal
eclipse (n.) darkening; covering; diminishing; overshadowing
friction (n.) resistance; rubbing; conflict or disagreement between persons
fusion (n.) joining together of two pieces of metal or plastic by heating; blending
gravity (n.) pull of the earth; seriousness; significance
nucleus (n.) the center of a cell containing genes; central part of atom; core
orbit (n.) path of one heavenly body around another; track
organism (n.) cell; organic structure; living plant or animal
phenomenon (n.) an unusual event or happening; rarity; marvel
species (n.) category; classification; kind; breed
trait (n.) a distinguishing feature or characteristic; idiosyncrasy
velocity (n.) rapidity of motion; speed; momentum

Complete each sentence with the correct word from the box below.

evolved	astronomy	fusion	palpable	gravity
organism	traits	analyzed	verify	orbited
velocity	predict	porous	tepid	hypothesis
friction				

1. The student presented his _____ to the science chairman for approval.

2. It is easy to _____ the outcome when all the facts are known.

3. The students were asked to _____ their answers before submitting them.

4. _____ is the study of the science of the sky.

5. Static electricity is caused by _____.

6. The astronaut's craft _____ the earth several times prior to landing.

7. The rocket entered the earth's atmosphere with such _____ that its glow was evident in the night sky.

8. There is a(n) _____ difference in their athletic abilities.

9. The jeweler was able to repair the necklace using _____ to put the two pieces back together.

10. Parents pass on numerous _____ to their children.

11. You should wash your new T-shirt in _____ water.

12. The theme for the Spring Carnival _____ over many meetings.

13. A glass is not _____.

14. The scientist _____ the fossils to determine their age.

15. The evening weather report emphasized the _____ of the pending storm.

16. A human being is a complex _____.

Match the definition in Column 1 to the correct word from Vocabulary List 3 in Column 2.

Column 1

_____ 1. characteristic

_____ 2. the science of the planets and stars

_____ 3. obvious; noticeable

_____ 4. proposal

_____ 5. extremely dry

_____ 6. motionless

_____ 7. rapidity of motion

_____ 8. pull of the earth

_____ 9. resistance

_____10. indifferent

_____11. center of a cell

_____12. living thing

_____13. lethal

_____14. joining together

_____15. an unusual event

_____16. having to do with the stars

_____17. guess

_____18. path of a heavenly body

_____19. overshadowing

_____20. type

Column 2

a. tepid

b. organism

c. astronomy

d. arid

e. inert

f. toxic

g. nucleus

h. palpable

i. phenomenon

j. orbit

k. velocity

l. hypothesis

m. fusion

n. species

o. gravity

p. conjecture

q. eclipse

r. trait

s. friction

t. celestial

Complete the passage below using words from Vocabulary List 3.

A "Moving" Experience

Our journey began innocently enough with the typical shudder and intense roar of the Saturn rockets as we lifted off. The tension in the air was (1)_____ as the craft fought Earth's (2)_____.

We all had (3)_____ our own theories as to what we would experience on this, our maiden voyage to the (4)_____ world. During the weeks prior to boarding, our family had read all we could on the area we would be visiting. We had also spoken to others recently returned from similar voyages. We (5)_____ the information and formulated the best plan for us.

There were so many questions. Would there be (6)_____ deserts? Would we need to wear oxygen masks due to (7)_____ gasses? Would there be life, or had it disappeared due to (8)_____ conditions on the surface? Would our clothing be so (9)_____ that harmful (10)_____ could make their homes there?

After all the planning, our concerns proved unnecessary, though there were a few hair-raising moments as we entered the planet's (11)_____. All too soon, our ship descended with terrific (12)_____. The (13)_____ caused by entering the alien atmosphere made the inside of the capsule glow intensely. Landing was imminent. Finally, the all-safe button flashed, and we were able to disembark.

Our first view was (14)_____ by the forms of shadowy figures; friendly, but no doubt another (15)_____. They could not possibly be human! Their words drifted through the mist, "We hope you enjoyed your flight. Have a nice day."

Yea! Only 15 more Disneyland rides to tackle. Onward, brave family!

Words and numbers rule

Power up—use your writer's tricks

analogy (n.) similarity; comparison
connotation (n.) insinuation; suggested meaning; implication
denouement (n.) final solution of the plot of a book; outcome; end
literal (adj.) the actual dictionary meaning of a word; exact; precise
nuance (n.) slight shade, degree, or hint of difference in meaning; suggestion
paradox (n.) riddle; enigma; a self-contradictory statement
pseudonym (n.) a pen name; a false name used by an author; alias
pun (n.) use of a word so as to suggest different meanings; double meaning

To tell your tale

allegory (n.) a story in which people and events have a symbolic meaning
anecdote (n.) a short story about an incident in someone's life
myth (n.) a story that tells about gods and goddesses; false idea that people believe
parable (n.) a short story designed to teach a moral or spiritual lesson
saga (n.) long, detailed story; epic; legend; history
satire (n.) parody; mockery; ridicule; comic criticism

Become a math expert

adjacent (adj.) close to or next to; bordering; contiguous
approximate (adj.) nearly correct or exact; estimated
estimate (v.) roughly guess or calculate; evaluate; figure
infinite (adj.) without end; boundless
perimeter (n.) the outside edge of an area; distance around the edge of an area
perpendicular (adj.) a line at right angles to another line; vertical; upright
prime (adj.) having no factor except itself and one; first in importance
random (adj.) having no pattern or reason; unintended; accidental
tangible (adj.) able to be touched or felt; verifiable; definite
variable (n.) a symbol or quantity whose value can change
vertical (adj.) going straight up and down; steep

Solve the crossword puzzle below using words from Vocabulary List 4.

Across

1. short story about someone's life
3. outcome
4. unplanned
7. riddle
8. insinuation
11. going straight up and down
13. symbol whose value can change
15. next to
16. roughly guess

Down

1. symbolic story
2. comparison
5. shade of meaning
6. double meaning
7. first
9. verifiable
10. parody
12. story that teaches a moral lesson
14. false idea people believe

Choose the correct word from Vocabulary List 4 for each item.

_____ 1. enigma

    a. pun
    b. nuance
    c. paradox

_____ 2. accidental

    a. vertical
    b. estimate
    c. random

_____ 3. nearly correct

    a. analogy
    b. approximate
    c. estimate

_____ 4. a symbol whose value changes

    a. anecdote
    b. variable
    c. infinite

_____ 5. shade of meaning

    a. prime
    b. literal
    c. nuance

_____ 6. symbolic story

    a. allegory
    b. analogy
    c. connotation

_____ 7. able to be felt

    a. perpendicular
    b. tangible
    c. parable

_____ 8. next to

    a. perimeter
    b. perpendicular
    c. adjacent

_____ 9. without end

    a. denouement
    b. literal
    c. infinite

_____ 10. first in importance

    a. prime
    b. myth
    c. pseudonym

_____ 11. going straight up and down

    a. variable
    b. vertical
    c. conjecture

_____ 12. evaluate; calculate

    a. myth
    b. literal
    c. estimate

_____ 13. epic; history

    a. anecdote
    b. satire
    c. saga

_____ 14. outer boundary

    a. perimeter
    b. saga
    c. eclipse

_____ 15. comparison

    a. pseudonym
    b. analogy
    c. denouement

_____ 16. lines meeting at right angles

    a. tangible
    b. perpendicular
    c. adjacent

Choose the correct word from Vocabulary List 4 for each item and circle it in the word search below.

A	I	Y	M	D	T	M	Y	N	O	D	U	E	S	P
N	X	W	X	Z	F	E	T	I	N	I	F	N	I	E
E	Q	O	D	F	W	M	F	S	T	W	Y	R	C	A
C	E	Y	D	C	E	F	A	L	R	Q	A	N	P	B
D	F	F	Z	A	O	X	V	W	M	G	A	P	I	V
O	B	A	G	A	R	N	T	A	A	U	R	S	P	L
T	X	U	R	A	Q	A	N	S	N	O	O	J	R	H
E	W	H	U	N	Y	U	P	O	X	L	Q	V	V	C
V	V	T	R	Q	B	F	L	I	T	O	U	D	B	C
R	V	I	W	G	O	I	M	F	S	A	H	T	K	K
Z	C	N	B	Q	T	A	T	J	N	A	T	S	Y	N
I	I	M	U	E	T	B	I	N	P	Q	T	I	I	Q
B	U	K	R	E	F	T	D	A	E	G	H	I	O	G
D	D	A	M	U	N	P	D	S	M	Z	Y	N	R	N
J	L	P	U	N	B	V	J	B	E	I	V	U	C	E

1. brief story

2. an implication

3. exact meaning

4. epic

5. ridicule

6. nearly exact

7. without end

8. author's pen name

9. double meaning

10. shade of meaning

11. riddle

Investigate your future

Discover the world of government

abdicate (v.) resign; formally give up power or responsibility
allegiance (n.) loyalty to a nation or a cause; deep commitment
amend (v.) improve; change; revise; remedy; fix
anarchy (n.) total absence of government and law; confusion; disorder
annex (v.) add to; attach; add to one's territory to form a larger country
decree (n.) an official order or decision from someone in authority
defect (v.) desert a cause, organization, or country in order to join another
immigrant (n.) one who comes to a country to live there permanently
legacy (n.) heritage; tradition; inheritance
nomad (n.) one who wanders from place to place and has no fixed home
ratify (v.) confirm; approve; authorize
realm (n.) a kingdom; a region or field of study
resolution (n.) a formal proposition or proposal; firmness of purpose; answer
tyranny (n.) very cruel and unjust use of power or authority; absolute rule

Feel the pulse of the business world

agenda (n.) a list of things to be considered or done; schedule
apprentice (n.) one who learns a trade by working with a skilled person; beginner; tyro
bias (n.) prejudice; bigotry; inclination; fixed idea; narrow view
boycott (v.) refusing to deal with; exclude
consolidate (v.) unify; incorporate; merge; strengthen; solidify
diversity (n.) difference; variety
embargo (n.) order forbidding the trade in commercial goods; restriction
entrepreneur (n.) one who begins or takes on the risk of a business
expenditure (n.) spent money, time, or energy; expenses
incentive (n.) something that makes a person want to try or work harder; inducement
revenue (n.) income received from taxes; salary; profit

Match the definition in Column 1 to the correct word from Vocabulary List 5 in Column 2.

Column 1

_____ 1. learner; beginner

_____ 2. a wanderer

_____ 3. inducement

_____ 4. cruel use of power

_____ 5. formally give up power

_____ 6. one who takes a business risk

_____ 7. desert a cause

_____ 8. attach; add to

_____ 9. kingdom

_____10. deep commitment

_____11. one who leaves his country

_____12. heritage; tradition

_____13. order restricting trade

_____14. change; improve

_____15. variety

_____16. list of things to do

_____17. income

_____18. an official order

_____19. authorize

_____20. narrow view

Column 2

a. tyranny

b. defect

c. apprentice

d. amend

e. ratify

f. abdicate

g. allegiance

h. entrepreneur

i. bias

j. embargo

k. nomad

l. realm

m. agenda

n. incentive

o. legacy

p. revenue

q. annex

r. decree

s. diversity

t. immigrant

Complete each headline by circling the correct word.

1. Pizza _____ a Success: Students Read 5,000 Books

   Incentive   Bias   Revenue

2. Surfboard Factory Opens: _____ Needed

   Defect   Embargo   Apprentices

3. PTA _____: Plan Student Input

   Consolidation   Agenda   Entrepreneur

4. South America Focus on _____ Day

   Resolution   Boycott   Diversity

5. King Dismisses Government: _____ Follows

   Incentive   Anarchy   Expenditure

6. Parents Support Students' Video Store _____

   Abdication   Embargo   Boycott

7. Budget Deficit: Club's _____ Questioned

   Expenditures   Agenda   Diversity

8. Hot Dog Sales _____ Up: New Team Uniforms in Future

   Tyranny   Revenue   Legacy

Replace each bold word with a word from the box below with the same meaning.

defect	allegiance	amended	diversity	decreed
legacy	nomads	ratify	realms	embargo
revenue	incentive	resolution	consolidate	entrepreneurial

1. There is grave concern that many musicians will **leave** in order to study in less oppressive conditions.

2. The children's **managerial** future was seen in their sidewalk lemonade stand.

3. Eye contact was all the **motivation** my dog needed to jump on my lap.

4. Show **loyalty** to your country by honoring its flag.

5. The **revised** edition of my novel was finally accepted for publication.

6. We were thrilled when the principal **proclaimed** Tuesday as a "no homework" day.

7. The greatest **inheritance** a parent can leave his children is a sense of morality.

8. Early Native Americans were **wanderers**, moving with the herds of buffalo.

9. We hope the Senate will **approve** the President's choice for Secretary of Education.

10. It is interesting to learn about the various geographical **regions**.

11. It is rewarding to live in a community that celebrates its cultural **differences**.

12. The **profits** from the car wash helped to defray the costs of our class trip.

13. One day there may be a **ban** against gasoline-operated cars in favor of those fueled by solar power.

14. Have you ever made a New Year's **promise**?

15. If we win this game, it will **strengthen** our team's chance to go to the state finals.

Write Yes if the vocabulary word is used correctly and No if it is not.

_____ 1. A **genial** person will find it difficult in a new school.

_____ 2. Wearing mismatched socks is a **peculiar** habit.

_____ 3. A **competent** student strives to complete all assignments on time.

_____ 4. Teachers want essays which make little use of **clichés**.

_____ 5. You will learn to snowboard if you **persevere**.

_____ 6. **Persistence** is a trait to be avoided.

_____ 7. Lasting friendships **evolve** over time.

_____ 8. An **arid** climate is needed for a green lawn.

_____ 9. Today's top rock star's fame may easily be **eclipsed** by an unknown musician.

_____ 10. Some authors choose to use a **pseudonym** when writing a novel.

_____ 11. A **myth** is a brief biography about a famous person.

_____ 12. Many pet owners place an invisible fence along the **perimeter** of their property.

_____ 13. One way of showing consumer approval is by **boycotting** a product.

_____ 14. An **entrepreneur** takes few risks when setting up a new business.

_____ 15. Each winter, **immigrants** travel to warmer climates to escape the winter cold.

_____ 16. **Boisterous** fans ruin the game for everyone.

_____ 17. A well-written science paper is enhanced by the use of **puns**.

_____ 18. Some people believe they can **predict** their future by reading the stars.

_____ 19. There are an **indefinite** number of students in our school.

_____ 20. A ruler's **tyrannical** regime could start a revolution among his subjects.

Use words from Vocabulary Lists 1–5 to find the hidden message.

1. _ _ ◯ _ _ _   official order

2. _ _ _ _ ◯ _   parody; ridicule

3. _ _ _ ◯ _ _ _ _ _   motivation

4. _ _ ◯ _ _ _ _ _   come to grips with

5. _ _ ◯ _ _ _ _ _   sensible; reasonable

6. _ _ ◯ _ _ _ _   anticipate; guess in advance

7. _ _ _ ◯ _ _ _ _   close to; next to

8. _ _ _ _ ◯ _ _ _   without end

9. _ ◯ _ _ _ _   similarity

10. _ ◯ _ _ _ _ _   order forbidding trade

11. _ _ _ _ _ ◯ _ _ _ _ _   unplanned

12. _ _ _ _ _ ◯ _   study something carefully

13. _ _ _ ◯ _   causing harm; lethal

14. _ _ _ _ ◯   want; pine for

15. ◯ _ _ _ _ _   sociable

16. _ _ _ _ _ ◯◯   cheerful

17. _ _ _ _ _ ◯ _ _ _   impossible to read

18. _ _ _ ◯ _   establish the truth of

19. _ ◯ _ _ _ _   nerve; fortitude

Hidden Message: "_ _ _ _ _ _   _ _   _ _ _ _ _ _ _
                      1 2 3 4 5 6   7 8   9 10 11 12 13 14 15

_ _ _ _."
16 17 18 19

Match the word from Vocabulary Lists 1–5 (Column 1) with the word or phrase with the opposite meaning (Column 2).

Column 1

_____ 1. incoherent

_____ 2. assert

_____ 3. perceive

_____ 4. motivated

_____ 5. infinite

_____ 6. random

_____ 7. tyranny

_____ 8. nucleus

_____ 9. consolidate

_____10. palpable

_____11. celestial

_____12. perimeter

_____13. oblivious

_____14. tangible

_____15. conjecture

_____16. bias

_____17. incomprehensible

_____18. inert

_____19. monotonous

_____20. mingle

Column 2

a. planned

b. based on fact

c. aware

d. limited

e. avoid

f. ignore

g. separate

h. understandable

i. fairness

j. immaterial; ethereal

k. center

l. unnoticeable

m. interesting

n. discouraged

o. outer shell

p. earthly

q. democracy

r. energetic

s. deny

t. logical; connected

Complete each sentence by circling the correct word from Vocabulary Lists 1–5.

1. The biologist discovered a new (species, nucleus) of fish while diving in an underwater cave.

2. The jet's (fusion, velocity) enabled it to break the sound barrier.

3. The toddler's (inquisitive, biased) nature exhausted everyone with his incessant "Why, why?"

4. Five powerful hurricanes are (predicted, decreed) for this season.

5. The popular (satire, connotation) of the word *cool* has nothing to do with temperature.

6. I won't recommend this novel to anyone; its (prediction, denouement) was too disappointing.

7. Tiger Woods was considered a golfing (phenomenon, apprentice) at an early age.

8. Parents hope their children will emulate their more positive (traits, pseudonyms).

9. The anti-government crowd called for the (annexation, abdication) of the czar.

10. The administration passed a(n) (embargo, resolution) calling for more protein choices during lunch.

11. During the Great Famine, thousands of Irish (immigrants, entrepreneurs) left their country to make a new life in the United States.

12. When Dad discussed his company's (collaboration, consolidation) plans, we became concerned he would lose his job.

13. Both teams are so good I wouldn't want to (speculate, assert) about the outcome of the series.

14. Our class trip was postponed (monotonously, indefinitely) due to severe weather.

15. It was impossible to stifle a yawn as the candidate's speech disintegrated into one (rambling, reflective) thought after another.

16. Our school opened its planetarium to the public; now all can participate in (mythological, celestial) studies.

Choose the correct word from Vocabulary Lists I–5 for each item and complete the wheel below. The last letter of each word is the first letter of the word that follows.

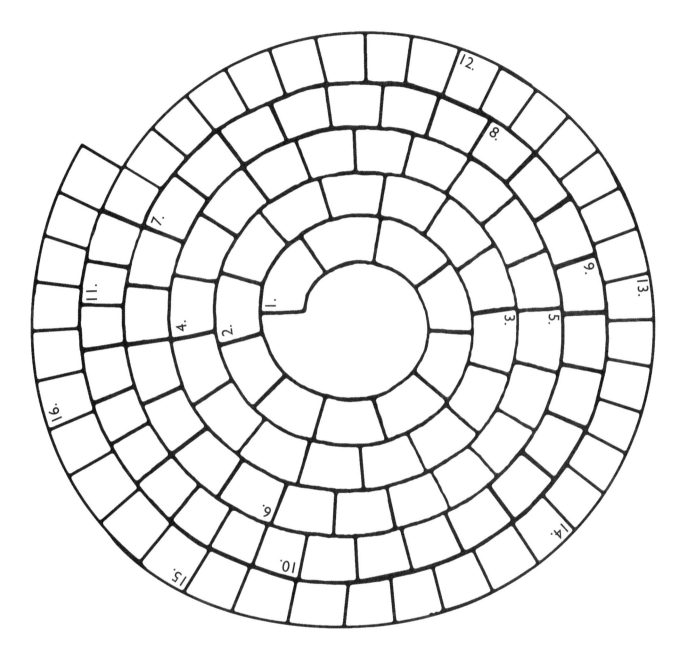

1. look forward to
2. persuasive; stirring
3. timid; shaky
4. easily influenced
5. roughly guess or calculate
6. restriction
7. living plant or animal
8. false idea that people believe

9. assumption; proposal
10. wonder about a subject
11. one who begins a business
12. talk without a clear purpose
13. confused; distorted
14. difference; variety
15. want; crave
16. slight difference in meaning

Solve the crossword puzzle below using words from Vocabulary Lists 1–5.

Across

1. refuse to quit
5. schedule
8. baffling
13. inactive
15. blending
17. beginner

Down

2. expand
3. epic
4. assumption; guess
6. adjust
7. science of stars and planets
8. unable to read
9. absorbent
10. proposal
11. establish the truth of
12. excited
14. desert a cause
16. track

Your home

A place of...

affirmation (n.) approval; confirmation; endorsement
assent (n.) agreement; acceptance; approval; acknowledgement
asylum (n.) shelter; place of safety; protection given, especially to political refugees
refuge (n.) shelter or protection from danger; haven
respite (n.) a period of rest; intermission; a pause; reprieve; delay
sanctuary (n.) a safe place; protection; preserve; a holy or sacred place
solace (n.) comfort in times of grief or worry; help in need

Protection from...

calamity (n.) deep distress; disaster; catastrophe; hardship
folly (n.) lack of good sense or judgment; a foolish act or idea; silliness
jeopardy (n.) peril; danger; risk of loss from injury
peril (n.) being in danger of injury or destruction; vulnerability
plight (n.) difficult or dangerous condition or situation; crisis; predicament
woe (n.) great sadness, suffering, or misfortune; worry

Your room perhaps?

adequate (adj.) sufficient; enough; satisfactory
capacious (adj.) roomy; spacious; ample; huge
chaos (n.) confusion; disorder; disorganization; mess
drab (adj.) lacking variety and interest; dull; dingy; cheerless
immaculate (adj.) perfectly clean; spotless; without a flaw
jumble (n.) confusion; disarray; clutter; hodgepodge
labyrinth (n.) maze; something extremely complicated or twisting; tangle
marvel (n.) something that causes wonder or astonishment; miracle; rarity
maze (n.) something very mixed up and confusing; labyrinth
spacious (adj.) large; wide; sizeable; roomy; not crowded
unique (adj.) one of a kind; unequaled; unusual; distinctive
unkempt (adj.) untidy as a result of neglect; disordered

Choose the correct definition for each word from Vocabulary List 6.

_____ 1. peril
    a. being in danger
    b. satisfactory
    c. approval

_____ 2. asylum
    a. confirmation
    b. preserve
    c. protection given to refugees

_____ 3. sanctuary
    a. a safe place
    b. peril
    c. foolish act

_____ 4. refuge
    a. shelter
    b. word for word
    c. official order

_____ 5. capacious
    a. great suffering
    b. roomy
    c. confirm

_____ 6. respite
    a. difference
    b. desert a cause
    c. intermission

_____ 7. folly
    a. inducement
    b. foolish act
    c. improve

_____ 8. jeopardy
    a. desert a cause
    b. peril
    c. narrow view

_____ 9. unkempt
    a. preserve
    b. untidy due to neglect
    c. without a flaw

_____ 10. calamity
    a. sufficient
    b. disaster
    c. protection

_____ 11. marvel
    a. miracle
    b. cheerless
    c. difference

_____ 12. affirmation
    a. hardship
    b. sufficient
    c. confirmation

_____ 13. woe
    a. desert a cause
    b. difficult situation
    c. great suffering

_____ 14. solace
    a. a sacred place
    b. comfort in times of grief
    c. foolish act

_____ 15. assent
    a. distinctive
    b. approval
    c. delay

_____ 16. plight
    a. difficult situation
    b. disaster
    c. disorder

An **analogy** expresses a similar relationship between two words or phrases. Following is an example of how an analogy is written and how that same analogy is read.

HOT : COLD :: NIGHT : DAY

HOT is to COLD as NIGHT is to DAY.

Complete the following analogies.

_____ 1. SANCTUARY : SOLACE ::

    (a) folly : peril   (b) woe : solace   (c) plight : labyrinth

    (d) maze : refuge   (e) asylum : respite

_____ 2. IMMACULATE : UNKEMPT ::

    (a) drab : marvel   (b) grapple : illegible   (c) adequate : spacious

    (d) capacious : unique   (e) sanctuary : solace

_____ 3. FOLLY : CALAMITY ::

    (a) marvel : nomad   (b) plight : woe   (c) jeopardy : maze

    (d) labyrinth : resolution (e) lampoon : rescind

_____ 4. AFFIRMATION : ASSENT ::

    (a) peril : defect   (b) drab : adequate   (c) refuge : bias

    (d) maze : labyrinth   (e) jeopardy : calamity

_____ 5. MARVEL : UNIQUE ::

    (a) tyranny : dubious   (b) infinite : saga   (c) jumble : chaotic

    (d) random : anecdote   (e) spacious : capacious

Complete the passage below using words from Vocabulary List 6.

No Man's Land

It was Brittany's tale of woe, recounted from school by cell phone, that provided a slight (1)_____ from her mother's everyday (2)_____ routine in Normalville. Brittany had described her terrible (3)_____, "...on the desk in my room is the most (4)_____ CD in the world. My social life will be in total jeopardy if I can't get it by sixth period!" Brittany's mother recognized the peril facing her; she had just received consent to enter her daughter's room—a refuge which had long provided (5)_____ in times of chaos, a private sanctuary unseen by adults for centuries! Would it be a(n) (6)_____ to retrieve the CD even with a cell phone (7)_____ to enter the room? Was this permission adequate to avoid some great calamity behind the door bearing the sign "Brittany's Land of Marvel"?

She walked slowly down the (8)_____ hallway toward the room. Would she find an unkempt and crowded (9)_____ of clothes, furniture, and electronic gear? Must she fight through a maze of pizza crusts and rock concert posters? Slowly she opened the door and whispered, "He-l-l-o-o-o. I'm just coming in to get Brittany's CD on her desk, OK?" She was surprised to see a pleasant and capacious area that was absolutely (10)_____, except for a soda can on the desk. "You're cool, Mrs. Stewart...and expected," a quiet voice said. The soda can picked up the CD in its hands ("*Hands?*" thought Mrs. Stewart), hopped over to where she stood, and gave it to her with a smile.

Mrs. Stewart suddenly awoke. She had fallen asleep in her home office—her own peaceful (11)_____ far from the outside world—a lovely (12)_____ of clothes, furniture, and electronic gear. "*Whew! Only a dream!*" she thought with relief. Then the telephone rang, and Brittany sounded happy. "Great job, Mom! Without you I would have been toast!" Mrs. Stewart almost dropped the phone in disbelief. *Had* it been a dream? But...a talking soda can?

Family matters

The grown-ups around you should...

foster (v.) encourage; aid; nurture; support; side with
implore (v.) beseech; plead with
impose (v.) enact; establish; dictate
instill (v.) teach; impart; inspire
persuade (v.) influence; talk into; coax; tempt
probe (v.) inquire; question; examine; investigate thoroughly; explore
reassure (v.) encourage; cheer up; comfort; assure
reprimand (v.) scold; find fault with; reproach; rebuke

And your siblings may...

astonish (v.) surprise; amaze; startle; shock; bewilder
bellow (v.) yell; bawl; roar; shriek; shout
clamor (v.) shout; cry out; make a racket; demand something noisily
divulge (v.) tell; reveal; make public; disclose
quibble (v.) bicker; raise trivial objections; split hairs
squabble (v.) quarrel; dispute; differ; argue

Your sibs could also be...

abrupt (adj.) rudely brief; blunt; impolite; sudden; unexpected
exasperating (v.) irritating; annoying; aggravating
exhausting (v.) very tiring, wearing, and/or draining; using up completely; depleting
extraordinary (adj.) so unusual as to be remarkable; amazing; strange
frank (adj.) direct; outspoken; honest; unambiguous
tolerant (adj.) understanding; fair; lenient; patient

So it's up to you to...

compromise (v.) settle a dispute by giving up some demands; risk; endanger
concur (v.) act together; be in agreement
entreat (v.) ask earnestly; beg; plead with
rectify (v.) make right; correct; remedy
succumb (v.) give in; yield; comply with; defer to

Choose the correct word from Vocabulary List 7 for each item and circle it in the word search below.

M	I	P	E	R	S	U	A	D	E	S	Y	P	I	E
S	G	M	S	F	X	Z	M	S	U	K	P	M	L	A
B	U	N	P	Y	U	U	O	Z	B	V	P	B	E	S
L	T	C	I	L	P	Z	X	P	B	O	B	X	C	T
L	O	T	C	T	O	S	W	U	S	I	T	S	R	O
D	L	A	S	U	S	R	G	E	U	R	F	C	A	N
D	E	V	H	Y	M	U	E	Q	A	A	M	A	J	I
N	R	U	T	I	P	B	A	O	E	I	X	G	L	S
A	A	M	U	G	I	B	R	H	R	L	D	A	J	H
M	N	F	Q	M	E	D	Q	Q	X	O	Z	R	J	U
I	T	C	C	L	I	W	L	Y	E	E	M	Y	Y	Z
R	Y	Q	L	N	M	M	D	N	Q	B	H	A	N	E
P	K	O	A	T	Z	H	P	R	P	B	O	V	L	M
E	W	R	J	P	G	C	M	R	L	R	C	R	E	C
R	Y	M	P	F	E	R	U	S	S	A	E	R	P	C

1. investigate thoroughly
2. shriek
3. demand something noisily
4. amazing
5. patient
6. give in
7. plead with

8. comfort
9. find fault with
10. amaze
11. raise trivial objections
12. very tiring
13. dictate
14. talk into

Write Yes if the vocabulary word is used correctly and No if it is not.

_____ 1. It is **exasperating** having to wait in line behind someone who is determined to pay their bill in coins.

_____ 2. An **abrupt** speech holds the attention of an audience.

_____ 3. A teacher's **frank** opinion about a science proposal is welcomed by serious students.

_____ 4. Parents should **succumb** to their teen's request for a late curfew.

_____ 5. You may be **exhausted** after a full day devoted to snowboarding.

_____ 6. It would be **extraordinary** if human life were found on Mars.

_____ 7. It is important to **rectify** your good deeds as soon as possible.

_____ 8. Scientists fly into a hurricane to **probe** its strength.

_____ 9. A **compromise** is one way to avoid an argument.

_____ 10. It is a good idea to prevent the **fostering** of widespread computer knowledge.

_____ 11. One should be **tolerant** of people who are bigoted and self-centered.

_____ 12. Honest Internet businesses should never ask you to **divulge** your private password.

_____ 13. Most people would **concur** that they prefer sunny days over thunderous ones.

_____ 14. **Squabbling** among friends is welcome at a party.

_____ 15. Many tennis players are successful because their parents **instilled** in them a love of the game at an early age.

Complete each sentence with the correct word from the box below.

squabbling	implored	reprimanded	probing	instilled
divulge	imposed	fostered	bellow	reassured
clamor	persuade	astonished	abrupt	concurs
exasperating	extraordinary			

1. Our experience with Little League _____ in us a spirit of fair play.

2. We _____ our teacher to let us have a "no homework day," but to no avail.

3. The principal _____ a stricter dress code because the students were dressing too casually.

4. Our parents _____ in us a sense of honesty at an early age.

5. She was finally able to _____ her mom to let her go to the mall with friends.

6. Our teacher's mood _____ us that our test results were _____.

7. The principal _____ those students who threw papers out of the school bus window.

8. Mark was _____ to learn he had been selected to represent our state at the National Skateboard Olympics.

9. When Sarah saw the spider on the wall near her desk, she let out a(n) _____ that could be heard in the next town.

10. My baby brother began to bang on his tray and _____ for more food.

11. If you know a secret that will harm another, you should _____ it.

12. Our family _____ that our next vacation should be near the ocean.

13. It was _____ that their _____ over who would drive made us late for the movie.

14. Her _____ question finally made me admit that I ate the whole pie.

15. He lost his job because of the _____ way he handled the customers.

It's My Party

Directions: Your job is to arrive at the party safely. Your route begins with Clue #1. Move up, down, left, right, and diagonally, but avoid the roadblocks!

			☆ folly			
asylum	assent	unique	folly	impose	solace	abrupt
asylum		affirmation	sanctuary	instill	divulge	unique
succumb	drab	folly	labyrinth	unkempt		folly
refuge	capacious	**PARTY**	spacious	quibble	capacious	quibble
rectify	chaos	tolerant	tolerant	chaos	solace	adequate
unique	affirmation	frank	immaculate	capacious	woe	concur
folly	divulge	reassure	spacious	marvel	friction	anecdote

Clues

1. silliness
2. distinctive
3. approval
4. shelter
5. yield
6. lacking variety
7. haven
8. mess
9. outspoken
10. understanding
11. spotless
12. miracle
13. misfortune
14. agree
15. enough
16. comfort
17. argue
18. untidy
19. tell
20. teach
21. maze
22. roomy

Complete each sentence with the correct word(s).

_____ 1. Last fall a local farmer cut a(n) _____ pattern into his wheat field; the _____ was then opened to the public.

(a) sanctuary...chaos   (b) extraordinary...myth   (c) unique...maze
(d) labyrinth...folly   (e) eminent...legacy

_____ 2. The Pyramids of Mexico are _____; visitors from around the world are amazed at their design.

(a) immaculate   (b) drab   (c) unkempt
(d) abrupt   (e) extraordinary

_____ 3. The birds of the rain forest are in great _____ as their habitat _____ to foresters and tourists.

(a) astonishment...probes   (b) calamity...reassures   (c) refuge...quibbles
(d) peril...succumbs   (e) resolution...divulges

_____ 4. Over-fishing of the sea has resulted in fewer fish in the nets; the fishermen's livelihoods may be in _____.

(a) affirmation   (b) respite   (c) refuge
(d) jeopardy   (e) eclipse

_____ 5. Perhaps she can be _____ to lend me her _____ handbag to use for my carry-on luggage.

(a) astonished...marvel   (b) persuaded...capacious   (c) implored...abrupt
(d) compromised...spacious   (e) entreated...exasperating

_____ 6. NASA's _____ landed on Mars and retrieved numerous samples from the planet's surface.

(a) probe   (b) asylum   (c) folly
(d) maze   (e) organism

_____ 7. Local teens offered to turn the _____ and _____ jumble of weeds and debris of a vacant lot into a playground for children.

(a) adequate...immaculate   (b) unique...abrupt   (c) marvelous...solace
(d) refuge...peculiar   (e) drab...chaotic

_____ 8. When my baby sister _____ for some ice cream we _____; if she finished her dinner she could have her choice of flavors.

(a) flustered...garbled   (b) implored...bellowed   (c) clamored...compromised
(d) quibbled...reprimanded   (e) divulged...agreed

The mall

Why go?

accumulate (v.) amass; collect; increase in amount; save up
acquire (v.) get; obtain; achieve; earn; get by one's own efforts
bestow (v.) award; confer; give; expend; devote
gratify (v.) indulge; please; satisfy; delight; entertain; amuse
haggle (v.) bargain with; barter; argue in a petty way; quarrel
relish (v.) enjoy greatly; appreciate
rendezvous (v.) meet by agreement; get together; gather

Hanging with your friends

amble (v.) walk leisurely; stroll; meander
loaf (v.) take it easy; do nothing; waste time
saunter (v.) walk in a casual and unhurried way; stroll
scurry (v.) move quickly and briskly; rush; scamper
stride (v.) take very long steps

Window shopping—the things you'll see

absurd (adj.) ridiculous; foolish; laughable; preposterous
conventional (adj.) normal; standard; traditional; accepted
exquisite (adj.) finely made; beautiful and delicate; superb; impeccable
frivolous (adj.) not worthy of serious attention; impractical; superficial
lavish (adj.) very costly; overly generous; extravagant; excessive
lustrous (adj.) sparkling brilliance; shiny; dazzling
ornate (adj.) elaborately decorated; fancy; flashy

Stop at the Food Court

delectable (adj.) delicious; highly pleasing; gratifying
entice (v.) attract; tempt; lure; persuade; coax
pungent (adj.) spicy; tangy in taste; strong-smelling
quench (v.) satisfy; extinguish; bring to an end
ravenous (adj.) hungry; famished; gluttonous; greedy; grasping
whet (v.) tempt; entice; stimulate; sharpen

Use words from Vocabulary List 8 to find the hidden message.

"What did the secretary think of her strict boss?"

1. __ __ __ __ __ ◯   award

2. __ ◯ __ __ __ __   bargain with

3. __ __ ◯ __ __ __   ridiculous

4. ◯ __ __ __ __ __ __   get

5. __ __ __ __ ◯ __ __   walk in a casual way

6. __ __ __ __ ◯ __ __ __ __   impractical

7. __ __ __ ◯ __ __ __   shiny

8. __ __ __ ◯ __ __ __   please; indulge

9. ◯ __ __ __ __   walk leisurely

10. __ __ __ ◯ __ __ __ __ __ __   get together

11. __ __ __ ◯ __ __   enjoy greatly

12. __ ◯ __ __ __ __   rush

Hidden Message: "He __ __ __ __ __ __ __ __ __ __ __ __."
                 1   9   3   2   10   11   12   5   4   8   6   7

Choose the correct word from Vocabulary List 8 for each item.

_____ 1. finely made

    a. ornate
    b. lustrous
    c. exquisite

_____ 2. indulge

    a. gratify
    b. bestow
    c. pungent

_____ 3. entice; stimulate

    a. acquire
    b. whet
    c. conventional

_____ 4. ridiculous

    a. conventional
    b. absurd
    c. amble

_____ 5. stroll

    a. stride
    b. absurd
    c. saunter

_____ 6. sparkling brilliance

    a. stride
    b. lustrous
    c. entice

_____ 7. spicy

    a. scurry
    b. delectable
    c. pungent

_____ 8. elaborately decorated

    a. amble
    b. exquisite
    c. ornate

_____ 9. satisfy

    a. loaf
    b. quench
    c. ravenous

_____ 10. attract; tempt

    a. bestow
    b. entice
    c. rendezvous

_____ 11. normal

    a. lavish
    b. conventional
    c. loaf

_____ 12. amass; collect

    a. scurry
    b. haggle
    c. accumulate

_____ 13. impractical

    a. ravenous
    b. rendezvous
    c. frivolous

_____ 14. delicious

    a. delectable
    b. frivolous
    c. quench

_____ 15. famished

    a. relish
    b. clamor
    c. ravenous

_____ 16. luxurious

    a. lavish
    b. acquire
    c. accumulate

Choose the correct word from Vocabulary List 8 for each item and circle it in the word search below.

L	O	S	D	Y	E	T	I	S	I	U	Q	X	E	E
D	A	T	N	R	V	S	O	N	M	V	E	J	L	B
W	B	V	W	H	E	T	T	M	S	E	Y	G	D	C
O	X	M	I	L	W	N	F	F	T	Q	G	F	N	P
D	P	J	M	S	E	O	D	A	T	A	F	F	Q	C
C	C	S	J	K	H	N	L	E	H	G	W	T	G	W
T	F	K	B	E	L	U	T	A	Z	V	S	L	J	S
P	E	H	Z	J	M	T	S	I	C	V	B	H	M	E
N	B	A	E	U	N	J	B	C	C	Q	O	I	L	H
T	X	L	C	E	H	E	T	E	U	E	U	U	B	D
E	Q	C	G	C	D	J	N	D	L	R	H	I	S	G
H	A	N	N	I	P	A	M	Z	W	O	R	P	R	J
W	U	E	R	R	Z	K	Q	E	M	E	M	Y	E	E
P	U	T	C	C	E	M	N	X	Q	Q	F	A	O	L
Q	S	R	A	V	E	N	O	U	S	M	Z	E	R	W

1. get by one's own efforts

2. meet

3. take it easy

4. rush

5. take long steps

6. finely made

7. extravagant

8. strong-smelling

9. famished

10. tempt

11. argue in a petty way

12. bring to an end

13. save up

14. coax

On the playing field

Make every play count

dexterous (adj.) skillful in use of hands; nimble; resourceful
fervent (adj.) very earnest; intense; eager; enthusiastic
flourish (v.) thrive; prosper; succeed; wave about in the air
painstaking (adj.) careful; thorough; conscientious
precise (adj.) exact; specific; accurate; careful; unbending
prevail (v.) succeed in convincing; triumph over; overcome
stamina (n.) vigor; endurance; energy; perseverance
versatile (adj.) having many different skills; talented; having many uses
vigorous (adj.) energetic; active; vibrant; powerful; aggressive

Cool moves

feint (n.) deliberately deceptive movement; a pretense; trick or bluff
intricate (adj.) complex; full of detail; difficult to understand
lithe (adj.) limber; supple; flexible; pliant; bending easily
maneuver (n.) clever or skillful move; tactic; military movement
nimble (adj.) agile; able to move quickly and easily; quickness of thinking
ruse (n.) an action designed to confuse or mislead; a scheme; a hoax

Nobody's perfect

blunder (v.) make a mistake through carelessness; stumble; slip up
botch (v.) bungle; make a mess of; spoil
forfeit (v.) lose; squander; waste
frenzied (adj.) very excited or upset; frantic; hysterical
haphazard (adj.) disorganized; unorganized; careless; unplanned
inept (adj.) incompetent; unqualified; inappropriate
sluggish (adj.) having little energy or activity; lethargic; listless
trifle (v.) treat lightly; toy; dawdle; waste time
ungainly (adj.) moving in an awkward or clumsy way
waver (v.) be doubtful; hesitate; find it hard to decide; sway; flutter

Complete each sentence with the correct word from the box below.

painstaking	fervent	ruse	flourish	nimble
intricate	stamina	vigorous	haphazard	forfeit
prevail	feint	blunder	versatile	inept
precise	maneuver	botched		

1. It was his _____ desire to attend the opening game at Yankee Stadium.

2. After Tom deleted critical documents, he had to _____ a week's salary; that _____ could have cost him his job.

3. The golfer drove the ball onto the green with a(n) _____ swing.

4. Your plants will _____ if given water and sunlight.

5. Olympic hopefuls will _____ if they have speed and _____.

6. Companies want to hire applicants who are _____.

7. Engineers must be _____ in their calculations in order to avoid a(n) _____ project.

8. Your poor decision was the result of _____ thinking and inadequate planning.

9. The naval officer was confident of the intricate _____ he had to perform.

10. Everyone saw the boxer's _____ to the right; no one was prepared for his left jab.

11. Father realized he was a victim of a(n) _____ but laughed it off.

12. With a(n) _____ move the deer jumped over the fence and ran across the road.

13. The driver was removed from his job because of his _____ attitude concerning driving infractions.

14. The girl took _____ care to braid her hair in a(n) _____ design.

Complete each sentence by circling the correct word.

1. The pitcher demonstrated his (precision, dexterity) by throwing balls with either arm.

2. The fans (maneuvered, flourished) their team's colors as the players ran onto the field.

3. The ice skater won a gold medal for her (intricate, botched) program.

4. We tried to trick our mom, but the (ruse, waver) did not work.

5. Their (vigor, blunder) on the field cost the team the championship.

6. Our opponents (relished, forfeited) the game because they did not arrive on time.

7. In a (frenzied, nimble) motion, the fish fought to get the food.

8. If you rush through the painting, you will end up with a (painstaking, botched) job.

9. The sloth is recognized as one of the most (sluggish, lithe) animals in the world.

10. It is unfair to (trifle, feint) with someone's offer of friendship.

11. Though the whale appears (inept, ungainly), it is amazing to watch this massive animal move its body through the water.

12. Once you have made up your mind about the trip, you should not (waver, prevail) in your decision.

Complete the passage below using words from Vocabulary List 9.

Mom to the Rescue

After painstaking efforts to reach the (**precise, inept**) angle where the remote could activate the monitor, it required only a (**blundering, dexterous**) twist of the boy's wrist to replace The Shopping Channel with *Revenge of the Mutant Leopards*. His father's immediate reaction was a sudden dive to the floor and a feint toward the chair, followed by a (**nimble, painstaking**) leap over the table that brought *his* remote into position. Immediately, (**lithe, sluggish**) leopards were replaced by a man screaming that "Only 25 pocket drills remain available, so act now!"

"Do not (**waver, trifle**) with me, young man!" roared his father. "You do not have the stamina to prevail. Your haphazard attempts to rule the TV are most (**intricate, inept**). Victory will be mine!" He stood and began to flourish his remote in a wave of celebration.

The boy understood that he could not (**prevail, waver**) but had to fight to the bitter end. He could not botch his next, and perhaps last, opportunity. He realized that only a clever ruse would overcome a vigorous opponent with a superior and (**versatile, ungainly**) offense. If he hesitated further, he would forfeit any hope of seeing if the mutant leopards were victorious. He chose the ultimate maneuver—the False Surrender. He stood up, placed his remote on the table, hung his head, and said in a(n) (**elated, fervent**) voice, "OK, Dad, you win. We'll watch your program." His hope that his father would blunder came true. His father made the fatal mistake of putting down his remote. In a flash, the boy seized it, removed the batteries, picked up his own remote, and aimed it at the pocket drill promoter. His father jumped toward the TV control panel but stopped in mid-leap as the front door opened.

The boy's mother looked at the results of their (**sluggish, frenzied**) struggle, sighed, and shook her head as several leopards began to eat a 747 jet plane. She pulled the plug.

Take time just for you

Time to...

seek an **alternative** (n.) choice; option; recourse
bolster (v.) support; reinforce; uphold; strengthen
clarify (v.) make easier to understand; explain; make pure or clear
contemplate (v.) give careful thought to; reflect upon; anticipate; plan
seek **inspiration** (n.) motivation; influence; incentive; creative thought
linger (v.) stay; wait; dawdle; procrastinate; survive; cling to life
muse (v.) meditate; consider; deliberate; reflect
recollect (v.) recall; remember
be **solitary** (adj.) all alone; lonely; isolated; secluded

Time for...

reverie (n.) daydream; meditation; preoccupation
solitude (n.) seclusion from others; isolation; lonely place
transition (n.) change; passage; transformation; progression
venture (n.) an undertaking involving risk, chance, or danger; fling

Then you'll be ready to...

accomplish (v.) achieve; succeed at; get done; finish; perform
commence (v.) make a beginning; start
endeavor (v.) try; work at; aspire; aim; do one's best
invincible (adj.) totally secure; incapable of being conquered; unbeatable
jar (v.) astound; stun; startle; vibrate harshly; agitate
be the **optimist** (n.) one who hopes for or expects the best
thrive (v.) do well; succeed; grow vigorously; bloom
unruffled (adj.) calm and unbothered; not even slightly disturbed; peaceful

Feelings

exhilaration (n.) elation; excitement; delight; joy
enthusiasm (n.) eagerness; anticipation; zest; interest; passion
replenished (adj.) revived; refreshed; made full or complete again; restocked
thoughtful (adj.) reflective; introspective; kind-hearted; considerate
transformed (adj.) changed completely; altered

Solve the crossword puzzle below using words from Vocabulary List 10.

Across

1. all alone
4. preoccupation
6. get done
10. choices
11. stay; wait
12. motivation
13. anticipate
15. strengthen
16. something that involves risk

Down

2. remember
3. change
5. try; work at
7. make clearer
8. changed completely
9. seclusion from others
14. meditate

Match the definition in Column 1 to the correct word from Vocabulary List 10 in Column 2.

Column 1

_____ 1. one who hopes for the best

_____ 2. choice; option

_____ 3. not even slightly disturbed

_____ 4. achieve; finish

_____ 5. change; passage

_____ 6. make easier to understand

_____ 7. kind-hearted; considerate

_____ 8. anticipation; eagerness; interest

_____ 9. do well; succeed

_____10. refreshed

_____11. excitement; elation

_____12. support; reinforce

_____13. work at; do one's best

_____14. make a beginning

_____15. startle; stun

_____16. stay; wait

_____17. seclusion from others

_____18. undertaking involving risk

_____19. unbeatable

_____20. recall; remember

_____21. altered

_____22. meditate; reflect

_____23. all alone

_____24. daydream

Column 2

a. accomplish

b. commence

c. enthusiasm

d. bolster

e. endeavor

f. thrive

g. linger

h. solitude

i. jar

j. replenished

k. unruffled

l. venture

m. alternative

n. exhilaration

o. optimist

p. recollect

q. transition

r. muse

s. reverie

t. thoughtful

u. clarify

v. transformed

w. solitary

x. invincible

Use words from Vocabulary List 10 to find the hidden message.

"What did the team shout as their goalie slipped in the mud, letting the opponent score a goal?"

1. __ __ ◯ __ __ __ __ __ __ __ __   change

2. __ ◯ __ __ __ __ __ __ __ __   calm and unbothered

3. __ __ __ __ __ ◯ __ __   isolation

4. ◯ ◯ __ __ __ __ __ __   undertaking involving danger

5. __ __ __ ◯ ◯ __ __ __   one who hopes for the best

6. __ ◯ __ __ __ __ ◯ __ __   recall

7. __ __ __ ◯ __ ◯ __ __   make a beginning

8. ◯ __ ◯ __ __ __ __   reinforce

9. __ __ ◯ __ __ __   succeed

Hidden Message: "Thanks for that __ __ __ __ __ __
                                   2   5   5   8   8   6

__ __ __ __ __ __ __ __."
7   I   7   6   3   4   4   9

Choose the correct synonym and antonym for each word from Vocabulary Lists 8–10.

POWer Word	S	A	Synonym	Antonym
1. acquire	____	____	A. give	a. awkward
2. entice	____	____	B. pointless; silly	b. discourage
3. relish	____	____	C. conscientious	c. simple
4. bestow	____	____	D. flavorful	d. unadorned
5. frivolous	____	____	E. take pleasure in	e. give up
6. conventional	____	____	F. calm; cool	f. unthinking
7. painstaking	____	____	G. usual	g. uncommon
8. dexterous	____	____	H. hang around	h. serious
9. intricate	____	____	I. deft	i. discouragement
10. blunder	____	____	J. full of detail	j. intentional
11. haphazard	____	____	K. flashy	k. soothe; calm
12. versatile	____	____	L. considerate	l. half-hearted
13. pungent	____	____	M. accomplished	m. limited
14. ornate	____	____	N. obtain	n. leave hastily
15. thoughtful	____	____	O. upset	o. be accurate
16. unruffled	____	____	P. creative thought	p. confuse
17. jar	____	____	Q. hit or miss	q. agitated
18. linger	____	____	R. make understandable	r. dislike
19. clarify	____	____	S. goof	s. tasteless
20. inspiration	____	____	T. attract	t. receive; acquire

Word Board Challenger

CLUES: definition, the list where the word is found, and the number of letters in the word; For example, the answer to Clue #1 (lustrous) is found in Vocabulary List 8 and has eight letters.

DIRECTIONS:

1. Player #1 writes the answer to a clue anywhere on the Word Board (see p. 59). Do not use a square with a value of 10 for the first move.
2. Each player in turn selects a clue and writes its POWer Word on the Word Board. All words must link crossword style.
3. Clues may be used only once and need not be solved in order. Not all clues will be used in every game.
4. Game is over once all clues, or as many as possible, are played.

SCORING: Players add up their scores. All values of letters, even those previously played, count. Winner has most points.

CLUES

1. dazzling (List #8; 8)
2. frantic (List #9; 8)
3. treat lightly (List #9; 6)
4. one who is hopeful (List #10; 8)
5. lost in thought (List #10; 7)
6. satisfy; indulge (List #8; 7)
7. do well (List #10; 6)
8. take long steps (List #8; 6)
9. energy (List #9; 7)
10. lose (List #9; 7)
11. consider (List #10; 4)
12. stroll (List #8; 5)
13. sharpen; stimulate (List #8; 4)
14. flexible (List #9; 5)
15. intense; eager (List #9; 7)
16. bring to an end (List #8; 6)
17. delight (List #10; 12)
18. trick; bluff (List #9; 5)
19. bargain with (List #8; 6)
20. accurate (List #9; 7)
21. revived; refreshed (List #10; 11)
22. preposterous (List #8; 6)
23. startle; stun (List #10; 3)
24. rush (List #8; 6)
25. a fling (List #10; 7)
26. waste time (List #8; 4)

Word Board

5					3		3					5
	4		10							10	4	
		3				4				3		
			2			1			2			
				1	4		4	1				
	10										10	
2					3	5	3					2
		5				1				5		
				1	10			1				
			2						10	2		
		3				4				3		
	4		10							10	4	
5					4			4				5

NOTE: The number in the square represents the value (number of points) of the letter written on that square.

Complete the following analogies.

_____ 1. BLUNDER : BOTCH ::

    (a) prevail : relish   (b) scurry : dexterous   (c) lavish : absurd
    (d) amble : saunter   (e) rendezvous : maneuver

_____ 2. ACCUMULATE : BESTOW ::

    (a) foster : implore   (b) loaf : scurry   (c) trifle : forfeit
    (d) delectable : relish   (e) ravenous : entice

_____ 3. VIGOROUS : SLUGGISH ::

    (a) precise : fervent   (b) accumulate : pungent   (c) whet : entice
    (d) nimble : ungainly   (e) ornate : lavish

_____ 4. DEXTEROUS : INEPT ::

    (a) exquisite : lavish   (b) delectable : ravenous   (c) satire : variable
    (d) lithe : versatile   (e) absurd : conventional

_____ 5. FEINT : RUSE ::

    (a) solitude : venture   (b) inspiration : alternative   (c) maneuver : gratify
    (d) estimate : persuade   (e) exhilaration : elation

_____ 6. CONTEMPLATE : MUSE ::

    (a) entreat : astonish   (b) endeavor : thrive   (c) grapple : cope
    (d) approximate : prime   (e) bolster : yearn

_____ 7. JAR : ASTONISH ::

    (a) quench : whet   (b) implore : accomplish   (c) linger : loaf
    (d) estimate : persuade   (e) exquisite : ornate

_____ 8. INVINCIBLE : WAVER ::

    (a) ravenous : precise   (b) entice : absurd   (c) fervent : prevail
    (d) vigorous : lavish   (e) solitary : mingle

Complete each of the following with a word from Vocabulary Lists 1–10.

1. __ __ __ __ C T __ __ __ __   delicious

2. __ __ __ D E __   think over

3. __ __ __ __ __ __ __ N C __   loyalty to a nation

4. __ __ __ M I __ __   endurance

5. __ A Z __   something mixed up

6. __ R I __   extremely dry

7. __ N V __ __ __ __ __ __ __   unbeatable

8. F L __ __ __ __ __ __   thrive

9. W A __ __ __   find it hard to decide

10. __ __ __ __ I O __ __   roomy

11. __ __ S C __ __ __ __ __ __ __   vulnerable

12. __ __ A L __   region; kingdom

13. __ N D __ __ __ __ __   do one's best

14. I N __ __ __ __ __ __ __ __ __   eager for knowledge

15. __ __ G A   long, detailed story

Match the word from Vocabulary Lists 1–10 (Column 1) with the correct definition (Column 2).

Column 1

_____ 1. anticipate

_____ 2. flustered

_____ 3. genial

_____ 4. inhibited

_____ 5. keen

_____ 6. query

_____ 7. irrelevant

_____ 8. analyze

_____ 9. nucleus

_____ 10. phenomenon

_____ 11. literal

_____ 12. analogy

_____ 13. annex

_____ 14. respite

_____ 15. jumble

_____ 16. ungainly

_____ 17. quibble

_____ 18. reassure

_____ 19. bestow

_____ 20. nimble

_____ 21. prevail

_____ 22. thoughtful

_____ 23. linger

_____ 24. alternative

Column 2

a. think through

b. pin hopes on

c. seek by asking

d. win out

e. heart of something; center

f. neighborly; lighthearted

g. confused

h. uptight

i. grab

j. quick-witted

k. another choice

l. remarkable

m. everything but the kitchen sink

n. unconnected

o. word-for-word

p. set one's mind at rest

q. breathing spell

r. klutzy

s. fleet-footed

t. comparison

u. hang around

v. considerate

w. hand out

x. raise trivial objections

Choose the correct word for each item.

_____ 1. alias

    a. peculiar
    b. pseudonym
    c. allegiance

_____ 2. something complicated and twisting

    a. garbled
    b. affirmation
    c. labyrinth

_____ 3. covering; diminishing

    a. incoherent
    b. eclipse
    c. calamity

_____ 4. category

    a. elated
    b. immaculate
    c. species

_____ 5. aggravating

    a. solitude
    b. transition
    c. exasperating

_____ 6. hoax; scheme

    a. maneuver
    b. ruse
    c. hypothesis

_____ 7. a list of things to be done

    a. precise
    b. agenda
    c. unique

_____ 8. bloom

    a. thrive
    b. eloquent
    c. enthusiasm

_____ 9. self-contradictory statement

    a. prevail
    b. asylum
    c. paradox

_____ 10. satisfactory

    a. adequate
    b. abrupt
    c. illegible

_____ 11. impart; inspire

    a. concur
    b. instill
    c. evolve

_____ 12. dictate

    a. probe
    b. apprentice
    c. impose

_____ 13. expenses

    a. expenditure
    b. resolution
    c. celestial

_____ 14. wave about in the air

    a. extraordinary
    b. rectify
    c. flourish

_____ 15. start

    a. commence
    b. succumb
    c. divulge

_____ 16. coax

    a. feint
    b. transformed
    c. persuade

Match the word from Vocabulary Lists 1–10 (Column 1) with the correct definition (Column 2).

Column 1	Column 2
_____ 1. solitude	a. slow; listless
_____ 2. transition	b. puzzled
_____ 3. contemplate	c. shelter
_____ 4. prevail	d. rarity; marvel
_____ 5. exhausting	e. overcome
_____ 6. chaos	f. labyrinth
_____ 7. foster	g. study hard for a test
_____ 8. implore	h. change; passage
_____ 9. maze	i. lines meeting at right angles
_____10. refuge	j. firmness of purpose
_____11. revenue	k. profit
_____12. perpendicular	l. badly written
_____13. ratify	m. give careful thought to
_____14. resolution	n. approve; authorize
_____15. phenomenon	o. mess; confusion
_____16. inert	p. encourage; support
_____17. illiterate	q. isolation
_____18. transcend	r. go beyond; rise above
_____19. perplexed	s. very tiring; draining
_____20. cram	t. plead with

Keeping great friends

Why you pick them

accord (n.) mutual understanding; agreement; willingness to do something
compassion (n.) sympathy; empathy; pity; mercy
discretion (n.) good sense in making decisions; good judgment; preference
disposition (n.) one's temperament; mood; tendency; inclination
empathy (n.) understanding; concern; caring; sensitivity
proficient (adj.) very capable; competent; expert; accomplished
proximity (n.) closeness; nearness
receptive (adj.) approachable; amenable; friendly; responsive
reciprocal (adj.) mutual; shared; interdependent
status (n.) one's position in relation to others; prestige; condition

But sometimes they...

baffle (v.) confuse; perplex; bewilder; astonish; stop; thwart
delude (v.) deceive; trick; lead into error; mislead
deprive (v.) take something away; confiscate; strip

Or sometimes they become...

a **braggart** (n.) boaster; big mouth
a **buffoon** (n.) course, stupid person; clown; prankster; fool
overbearing (adj.) domineering; bossy; arrogant
quirky (adj.) having an odd personal habit or idiosyncrasy; peculiar; eccentric
trying (adj.) hard to bear due to a strain on one's patience; irritating; annoying
zany (adj.) funny in a foolish, crazy way; nonsensical; inane

Friendship's ups and downs

diminish (v.) reduce; lessen; decline; wane; shrink
escalate (v.) intensify; grow rapidly; rise; soar; increase; advance
fluctuate (v.) keep changing; come and go; vacillate; waver; vary
forsake (v.) give up; renounce; leave; abandon; desert
mercurial (adj.) flighty; impulsive; erratic; fickle
turbulent (adj.) not smooth or calm; tempestuous; chaotic; unruly

List 11—Sentence Completion

Choose the correct word from the box below for each item.

forsake	discretion	buffoon	quirky	proximity
status	proficient	compassion	accord	deluding
disposition	reciprocal	baffling	fluctuates	turbulent
deprived				

1. The belligerent leaders offered to sit down to peace talks as a sign of their _____.

2. She volunteered to purchase the concert tickets because of her _____ to the arena.

3. It is important to show _____ to the elderly.

4. Use your _____ when you spend your allowance.

5. A pleasant _____ will win you many friends.

6. Her aversion to pizza is _____.

7. Spencer became a(n) _____ surfer after months of practice.

8. Their friendship is _____.

9. The _____ sea made our cruise an exciting one.

10. There is usually at least one _____ in each group.

11. Fish will not survive in a saltwater aquarium if the temperature _____ too much.

12. Her _____ habit of dying her hair orange baffled her parents.

13. We were _____ of our trip to Disneyworld because my little brother became ill.

14. You will only be _____ yourself if you think you can spend your life playing video games.

15. Some young people need the _____ that comes with wearing the latest logo design.

16. It is rude to _____ your old friends for new.

Solve the crossword puzzle below using words from Vocabulary List 11.

Across

2. vacillate; vary
6. boasters
7. concern
10. one's mood
12. approachable
13. eccentric
14. impulsive
15. annoying

Down

1. renounce
3. pity
4. funny in a foolish way
5. bossy
8. mutual understanding
9. confuse
10. shrink
11. not smooth or calm

Complete each sentence by circling the correct word.

1. My Dad and I are never in (accord, proficient) when it comes to sports.

2. Do not (forfeit, forsake) your elderly relations.

3. We were impressed with the young child's (overbearing, compassionate) nature.

4. Use your (discretion, status) when choosing videos.

5. Her sunny (disposition, turbulence) brought smiles to the faces of the nursing-home residents.

6. Dad thinks my friends are (reciprocal, zany), but he also knows they are good kids.

7. Their (mercurial, bragging) dispositions prevent them from making sound political judgments.

8. The mayor is concerned that the riots will (escalate, diminish).

9. The young star would not be (receptive, deprived) of her fifteen minutes of fame.

10. We were impressed by the level of (empathy, quirkiness) the young child demonstrated.

11. My brother has become (baffled, proficient) on the guitar.

12. My grandparents are pleased to be living in (proximity, empathy) to their children now that they are older.

13. My son's negative attitude about wearing a suit (baffles, boasters) me.

14. Do not (fluctuate, delude) yourself; there are more than a few calories in the jumbo hot fudge sundae.

15. There is a difference between being the class comic and the class (buffoon, compromiser).

These guys are unacceptable.

The "I'm better than you" crowd

elite (adj.) superior to others; most distinguished member of a group
imperious (adj.) domineering; overbearing; dictatorial
lofty (adj.) proud; haughty; scornful; aloof; superior; towering
ostracize (v.) exclude or keep out; shun; snub
sneer (v.) scorn; mock; disdain; belittle
swagger (v.) behave in a very proud manner; boast; strut

The bad guys

bigot (n.) one who is a prejudiced or a biased person
embezzler (n.) one who steals funds
hypocrite (n.) an insincere or two-faced person; a phony; fraud
manipulator (n.) one who uses trickery; one who intends to deceive
meddler (n.) one who interferes without right; one who pries
perjurer (n.) one who swears to a lie
slanderer (n.) one who discredits another by making false statements

The rude and nasty

curt (adj.) abrupt; blunt; so brief as to seem rude
gloat (v.) feel or show happiness or satisfaction in a mean way; revel in
impudent (adj.) rash; rude; disrespectful; brazen; impertinent
repulsive (adj.) disgusting; offensive; nasty; detestable; odious
uncouth (adj.) crude; not well-mannered; awkward; boorish; unrefined
unscrupulous (adj.) without moral principles; devious; unprincipled
unseemly (adj.) not proper or decent; unsuitable; undignified; offensive; vulgar

The poorly behaved

blameworthy (adj.) deserving blame; being at fault; culpable
insubordinate (adj.) not obeying authority; defiant; intractable; recalcitrant
obstinate (adj.) stubborn; inflexible; headstrong; unmanageable
rebellious (adj.) resistant; defiant; contrary; uncontrollable
unruly (adj.) disobedient; obstreperous; willful; having a lack of self-control

Complete each sentence with the correct word from the box below.

meddler	swaggering	perjurer	unruly	rebellious
gloat	impudent	unscrupulous	blameworthy	hypocrites
manipulated	lofty	insubordinate	unseemly	slander

1. The pirate had a(n) _____ walk.

2. The _____ toddlers refused to take their naps.

3. The angry student didn't think when he made the _____ remark.

4. _____ ideals are fine; practical ideas get the job done.

5. It is not proper to _____ at another's misfortune.

6. Some people are _____; they say one thing to you and another to someone else.

7. The lawyer's cross-examination exposed the _____'s false testimony.

8. The _____ crowd was asked to leave the stadium.

9. The _____ merchant raised his prices during the disaster.

10. The _____ officer was reprimanded.

11. Every student in the room was _____ for the disturbance.

12. The candidate felt that the local newspaper had _____ the facts.

13. Her _____ remarks were considered coarse and vulgar.

14. A(n) _____ is someone who pries into someone else's personal business.

15. _____ can destroy a person's character.

Match the word from Vocabulary List 12 (Column 1) with the correct definition (Column 2).

Column 1

_____ 1. unseemly

_____ 2. manipulator

_____ 3. uncouth

_____ 4. unruly

_____ 5. imperious

_____ 6. sneer

_____ 7. insubordinate

_____ 8. elite

_____ 9. curt

_____ 10. repulsive

_____ 11. obstinate

_____ 12. lofty

_____ 13. swagger

_____ 14. embezzler

_____ 15. impudent

_____ 16. bigot

_____ 17. unscrupulous

_____ 18. hypocrite

_____ 19. perjurer

_____ 20. gloat

_____ 21. blameworthy

_____ 22. ostracize

Column 2

a. being at fault; culpable

b. not proper or decent

c. domineering; overbearing

d. an insincere person

e. one who intends to deceive

f. abrupt; blunt

g. nasty; disgusting

h. show happiness in a mean way

i. belittle; mock

j. without moral principles

k. boast; strut

l. shun; snub

m. lack of self-control

n. inflexible; stubborn

o. disrespectful; impertinent

p. prejudiced person

q. one who swears to a lie

r. select few

s. not well-mannered

t. refusing to obey authority

u. one who steals money

v. aloof; superior

Choose the correct word from Vocabulary List 12 for each item and circle it in the word search below.

S	R	E	P	U	L	S	I	V	E	K	S	K	U	H
P	W	E	B	U	L	Y	I	H	X	H	A	N	Y	O
E	L	A	T	Q	Q	R	U	K	N	C	C	P	N	B
R	I	G	G	I	M	A	W	O	G	O	O	P	N	S
J	J	N	M	G	L	W	M	T	U	C	N	B	M	T
U	V	V	T	A	E	E	E	T	R	M	P	A	G	I
R	C	N	X	E	N	R	H	I	Y	R	Z	U	U	N
E	J	A	D	C	K	I	T	H	O	R	F	W	P	A
R	B	Z	G	A	O	E	P	J	V	W	S	Z	H	T
G	W	D	V	Y	B	H	A	U	Y	L	Q	I	Y	E
O	Z	L	T	I	X	O	Y	K	L	L	S	R	F	U
E	L	F	G	I	C	T	W	I	Y	A	U	R	O	B
Q	O	O	J	N	L	Y	T	S	O	U	T	R	H	Z
L	T	Z	A	P	X	A	P	F	O	R	F	O	N	A
I	M	P	E	R	I	O	U	S	U	R	O	S	R	U

1. a biased person
2. boast; strut
3. overbearing
4. not well-mannered
5. an insincere person
6. proud; aloof

7. headstrong
8. having a lack of self-control
9. offensive; detestable
10. superior to others
11. one who swears to a lie
12. trickster

Tune in to your feelings

Anger anyone?

aghast (adj.) astonished; shocked; struck with horror and dismay
indignation (n.) resentment; ire; fury; rage
infuriate (v.) make furious; enrage; madden; incense; provoke
smolder (v.) seethe; rage silently; fume; burn and smoke without flame
wrath (n.) forceful anger; fury; indignation

Just to annoy

berate (v.) scold sharply or harshly; reprimand
chafe (v.) irritate; vex; rub something in a way that causes it to become sore
harass (v.) pester; annoy or attack repeatedly
rankle (v.) cause anger, irritation, or bitterness; needle; rile; gripe

Deep sadness

brood (v.) worry; think long and anxiously about something
despair (v.) lose all hope or confidence; lose faith in
despondent (adj.) sad; without hope; discouraged
forlorn (adj.) unhappy; depressed; broken-hearted; deserted; solitary
wistful (adj.) mildly sad because of an unfulfilled wish or desire; regretful; longing
wretched (adj.) extremely unhappy; downcast; dejected; inferior; worthless

Strong dislike

deplore (v.) disapprove of strongly; feel or express sorrow or regret
detest (v.) dislike very strongly; hate
disdain (v.) look upon with scorn; despise
loathe (v.) feel intense dislike or disgust for; shrink from

Fearful

apprehension (n.) uneasiness; dread; anxiety; suspicion; concern; worry
cower (v.) crouch or shrink away from in fear and shame; grovel
cringe (v.) recoil; cower; flinch; grovel

Wow!

avid (adj.) eager; enthusiastic; having a strong desire for
awe (n.) respect and wonder; mixed feeling of terror, panic, and wonder
exuberant (adj.) joyously unrestrained and enthusiastic; full of life

Choose the correct word for each item.

_____ 1. dejected

    a. indignation
    b. wretched
    c. unruly

_____ 2. make furious

    a. avid
    b. infuriate
    c. smolder

_____ 3. uneasiness; dread

    a. apprehension
    b. wrath
    c. wistful

_____ 4. discouraged

    a. aghast
    b. brood
    c. despondent

_____ 5. look upon with scorn

    a. cower
    b. awe
    c. disdain

_____ 6. longing

    a. detest
    b. wistful
    c. berate

_____ 7. broken-hearted

    a. aghast
    b. despair
    c. forlorn

_____ 8. intense feeling of dislike

    a. harass
    b. loathe
    c. exuberant

_____ 9. lose all hope

    a. despair
    b. deplore
    c. cringe

_____ 10. amazed

    a. chafe
    b. aghast
    c. infuriate

_____ 11. forceful anger

    a. wrath
    b. obstinate
    c. brood

_____ 12. pester; annoy

    a. harass
    b. curt
    c. apprehension

_____ 13. scold sharply

    a. despondent
    b. rankle
    c. berate

_____ 14. rage silently

    a. smolder
    b. berate
    c. transform

_____ 15. disapprove of strongly

    a. despondent
    b. blameworthy
    c. deplore

_____ 16. resentment

    a. chafe
    b. harass
    c. indignation

Use words from Vocabulary List 13 to find the hidden message.

"What do people do when they become ill at a museum?"

1. __ __ __ __ __ __ __ ⃝ __ __ __   anxiety

2. __ ⃝ __ __ __ __ ⃝ __   disapprove of strongly

3. __ ⃝ ⃝ __ __ __ __   unhappy; depressed

4. __ __ __ ⃝ __ __ __   mildly sad; regretful

5. __ ⃝ __ __ ⃝ __   irritate; vex

6. __ __ __ __ ⃝ __   reprimand

7. ⃝ ⃝ __ __ __   shrink away in fear

8. __ __ ⃝ __ __ ⃝ ⃝ __ __   full of life

9. __ __ __ ⃝ __   fury; indignation

Hidden Message: "They go __ __   __ __ __   __ __ __
                            4 3   1 2 2   6 5 5

__ __ __ __ __ __ __."
 7 8 8 8 9 7 3

Solve the crossword puzzle below using words from Vocabulary List 13.

Across
2. rage silently
8. enthusiastic
9. uneasiness
12. feel intense disgust for
13. hate; dislike very strongly
14. shrink away in fear

Down
1. worry
3. lose all hope
4. recoil; flinch
5. cause irritation
6. resentment
7. regretful
9. respect and wonder
10. full of life
11. irritate

Getting along

What's the problem?

advice (n.) an offered opinion or suggestion; guidance
aggression (n.) hostile or aggressive behavior; a physical or verbal attack
allegation (n.) something stated without proof; assertion; claim
altercation (n.) a noisy or angry dispute; controversy; quarrel
avarice (n.) a strong desire for riches or possessions; greed; stinginess
controversy (n.) argument; dispute; altercation; dissension
fallacy (n.) false or mistaken idea, belief, or opinion; flaw in reasoning
feud (n.) a bitter, long-term quarrel; dispute
insinuation (n.) a suggestion or sly hint; implication; intimidation
notion (n.) idea; concept; suspicion; belief; opinion
perspective (n.) a point of view; outlook; prospect
revelation (n.) admission; discovery; disclosure

So...fix it!

acknowledge (v.) recognize the authority of; admit the truth of; reply to
convey (v.) transport; communicate; give; relate; transfer; consign
discern (v.) understand; comprehend; recognize as separate or different; see
discourse (n.) talk; conversation; lecture; dialogue
divert (v.) distract; turn from serious thoughts; change the direction of
enlighten (v.) inform; instruct; clarify; advise
impunity (n.) freedom from punishment, harm, or loss; absolution; exemption
oblige (v.) force; compel; demand of; earn gratitude of; do a favor for
refrain (v.) keep oneself from doing something; hold off; resist; refuse
relinquish (v.) renounce; put aside; give up; yield; quit; release; let go
solicit (v.) try to get something by asking; ask for; plead
terminate (v.) bring to an end; conclude; finish; discontinue
vindicate (v.) uphold; support; defend; corroborate; acquit

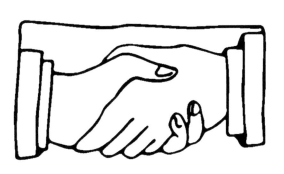

Complete each sentence with the correct word from the box below.

terminate	discern	acknowledged	impunity	divert
aggressively	insinuations	solicit	enlightening	altercation
relinquish	vindicate	obliged	conveyed	avaricious

1. To _____ the long family feud, both groups forgave each other's transgressions.

2. Her _____ nature was evident when we saw the amount of refundable bottles she had collected.

3. We were not allowed to _____ magazine subscriptions in the mall.

4. It is easy to _____ the facts of the case once the truth is known.

5. Once the district attorney became aware of the evidence, his only course was to offer _____ .

6. In order to _____ the sharp criticism, my opponent _____ took the offensive.

7. _____ of wrongdoing are as damaging as direct accusations.

8. The pilot _____ the directions of the control tower.

9. The teacher's presentation at the conference was _____ .

10. The _____ between the fans was quickly subdued.

11. The coach was asked to _____ his seat on the bus.

12. The lawyer asked the jury to _____ his client of the alleged charges.

13. Our family _____ our gratitude to the firefighter who rescued our cat from the tree.

14. We are _____ to pay taxes to support our government's programs.

Match the word from Vocabulary List 14 (Column 1) with the correct definition (Column 2).

Column 1

_____ 1. solicit

_____ 2. acknowledge

_____ 3. impunity

_____ 4. revelation

_____ 5. divert

_____ 6. perspective

_____ 7. discourse

_____ 8. aggression

_____ 9. discern

_____10. advice

_____11. convey

_____12. fallacy

_____13. feud

_____14. insinuation

_____15. notion

_____16. enlighten

_____17. vindicate

_____18. controversy

_____19. oblige

_____20. relinquish

Column 2

a. hostile behavior

b. admit the truth

c. dissention

d. ask for

e. guidance

f. flaw in reasoning

g. clarify; advise

h. belief

i. dialogue

j. exemption

k. do a favor for

l. point of view

m. release

n. suggestion; hint

o. prove correct

p. disclosure

q. transfer

r. see

s. turn from serious thoughts

t. long-term dispute

Choose the correct word from Vocabulary List 14 for each item and circle it in the word search below.

D	I	S	C	O	U	R	S	E	B	G	H	E	R	T
P	A	I	B	K	Q	B	R	H	H	N	C	R	E	E
S	D	Y	B	W	R	Q	F	J	O	I	R	M	F	R
R	C	O	S	Z	L	G	O	I	V	F	M	G	R	M
J	P	H	F	R	Y	R	T	D	S	C	B	R	A	I
O	R	L	K	Q	E	A	A	U	B	S	U	I	I	N
Q	R	G	E	V	G	V	T	T	S	T	Y	N	N	A
V	D	I	Q	E	A	H	O	N	T	E	M	H	G	T
P	Q	L	L	X	I	V	Y	R	R	R	F	N	I	E
G	I	L	D	F	A	D	K	L	T	E	E	M	A	A
G	A	U	K	R	S	Q	G	D	H	N	C	V	L	C
M	E	Q	M	I	A	F	V	K	M	F	O	S	I	Y
F	H	M	K	O	Y	C	A	L	L	A	F	C	I	D
O	T	Z	K	N	O	I	T	A	L	E	V	E	R	D
K	G	R	N	F	H	S	I	U	Q	N	I	L	E	R

1. opinion offered	7. keep from doing something
2. assertion; claim	8. talk
3. argument	9. distract
4. long-term quarrel	10. bring to an end
5. mistaken idea	11. understand
6. admission	12. put aside

Write Yes if the vocabulary word is used correctly and No if it is not.

_____ 1. Listening to rock music could be **trying** to some older folks.

_____ 2. One should use **discretion** when using a credit card.

_____ 3. An **overbearing** nature is necessary if you wish to make friends.

_____ 4. One way to involve new students in your school is to **ostracize** them.

_____ 5. Eating spaghetti with your hands is **uncouth** unless you are two years old.

_____ 6. **Unruly** children disturb other diners in a restaurant.

_____ 7. It is **infuriating** to share a locker with a sloppy friend.

_____ 8. **Avid** collectors seek any source to find what is needed for their hobby.

_____ 9. **Brooding** guests are the life of the party.

_____ 10. One should be cautious of giving unwanted **advice** or assistance.

_____ 11. **Allegations** of copying material from the Internet are serious.

_____ 12. One should **refrain** from eating breakfast.

_____ 13. An **altercation** between friends will strengthen their friendship.

_____ 14. Parents will be more **receptive** to suggestions presented clearly and calmly.

_____ 15. Only the **elite** are able to vote.

_____ 16. Coaches encourage their teams to **harass** the opponents.

_____ 17. You should **forsake** your old friends as you make new ones.

_____ 18. During disasters, donations are often **solicited** for the victims and their families.

_____ 19. One should **convey** good wishes to someone who has received an award.

_____ 20. You should **detest** broccoli because your friends do.

Use words from Vocabulary Lists 11–14 to find the hidden message.

1. __ __ __ ◯ __ __   prestige

2. __ __ ◯ __ __ __ __   stinginess

3. __ __ __ ◯ __ __ __ __   lose all hope

4. __ __ __ ◯ __ __ __   do a favor for

5. __ ◯ __ __ __ __   willful; disobedient

6. __ __ ◯ __ __ __   belief; opinion

7. __ __ __ __ __ ◯ __ __   coarse, stupid person

8. __ ◯ __   respect; wonder

9. __ __ __ __ ◯ __   fury; indignation

10. __ __ __ __ ◯ __ __ __ __   conversation

11. __ __ __ __ ◯ __   scornful; aloof

12. __ __ ◯ __ __ __ __ __ __   closeness

13. __ ◯ __ __   rudely brief

14. ◯ __ __ __   eager; enthusiastic

15. __ __ __ ◯ __ __ __   confiscate

16. ◯ __ __ __ __   superior to others

Hidden Message: " __ __ __   __ __ __ __   __ __ __
                         1   2   3   4   5   6   7   8   9   10

__ __ __   __ __ __ "
11 12 13   14 15 16

Complete the following analogies.

_____ 1. INFURIATE : SMOLDER ::

    (a) baffle : berate   (b) altercation : convey   (c) deplore : delude

    (d) insinuation : advice   (e) rankle : chafe

_____ 2. WRETCHED : EXUBERANT ::

    (a) imperious : sneering   (b) loathe : discern   (c) receptive : mercurial

    (d) inept : proficient   (e) despondent : wistful

_____ 3. BRAGGART : OVERBEARING ::

    (a) nomad : trying   (b) elite : curt   (c) zany : buffoons

    (d) rebels : lofty   (e) embezzler : unscrupulous

_____ 4. SLANDERER : COMPASSIONATE ::

    (a) meddler : unruly   (b) bigot : empathetic   (c) humdrum : cliché

    (d) infuriating : hypocrite   (e) persistent : manipulator

_____ 5. COWER : CRINGE ::

    (a) divert : brood   (b) ostracize : discern   (c) rebellious : insubordinate

    (d) altercation : disdain   (e) gloat : berate

_____ 6. INSINUATION : ALLEGATION ::

    (a) notion : discretion   (b) awe : wrath   (c) apprehension : avarice

    (d) solicit : precise   (e) controversy : feud

_____ 7. DISDAIN : DETEST ::

    (a) instill : relinquish   (b) perspective : stamina   (c) vindicate : assert

    (d) fluctuate : waver   (e) convey : terminate

_____ 8. DIMINISH : ESCALATE ::

    (a) ostracize : acknowledge   (b) baffle : forsake   (c) impudent : sneer

    (d) meddler : perjurer   (e) gloat : infuriate

Complete each sentence with the correct word(s).

_____ 1. In spite of her _____, Ellen never behaved in a(n) _____ manner.

    (a) discretion…compassionate   (b) deluding…turbulent   (c) quirky…obstinate
    (d) status…imperious   (e) proximity…discerning

_____ 2. If you show _____ to the elderly, they will be responsive to your sensitivity.

    (a) impunity   (b) disposition   (c) empathy
    (d) stamina   (e) tyranny

_____ 3. Where did you get the _____ that it was easy to learn to play the drums; such an idea would never be supported by a percussionist.

    (a) revelation   (b) notion   (c) feud
    (d) compassion   (e) allegation

_____ 4. He was ostracized by his neighbors because of his _____ and _____ behavior.

    (a) infuriating…invincible   (b) wistful…avid   (c) discretion…diverting
    (d) blameworthy…discerning   (e) impudent…repulsive

_____ 5. Seth is a _____ individual and would never be _____.

    (a) blameworthy…rebellious   (b) proficient…baffling   (c) receptive…insubordinate
    (d) quirky…zany   (e) lofty…bigoted

_____ 6. Your negative attitude will only _____ the feud, not _____ it.

    (a) escalate…diminish   (b) deplore…acknowledge   (c) solicit…terminate
    (d) harass…forsake   (e) botch…fluctuate

_____ 7. Her _____ behavior is _____.

    (a) brooding…exuberant   (b) elite…obstinate   (c) compassionate…zany
    (d) unscrupulous…unseemly   (e) aghast…forlorn

_____ 8. From my _____, the new stadium was poorly designed.

    (a) awe   (b) accord   (c) venture
    (d) inspiration   (e) perspective

Your music

For some it may be...

barrage (n.) words, noise, and sounds at the same time
interminable (adj.) endless; tediously long; continuous
irksome (adj.) annoying; tedious; causing boredom
prevalent (adj.) pervasive; widespread; commonly occurring; dominant
reverberate (v.) echo; resound; vibrate; boom
tumult (n.) commotion; racket; noise and confusion of a crowd

So they may then...

allot (v.) assign; allow; dispense; distribute
alter (v.) change partly but not completely; revise; modify
beseech (v.) ask earnestly for; beg; plead with; implore
compel (v.) force; require; limit choices
confiscate (v.) take possession of; appropriate; impound
dissuade (v.) discourage; advise against; urge not to
monitor (v.) watch; censor; oversee; guide
ration (v.) give out in restricted amounts
restrict (v.) limit; hamper; curb; hold back

But for you it's...

crucial (adj.) decisive; extremely important; essential; significant
novel (adj.) original; different; innovative; unconventional
pinnacle (n.) zenith; top; highest point of achievement
pivotal (adj.) the most important; critical; vital; crucial
predominant (adj.) major; supreme; important; influential
prominent (adj.) prestigious; eminent; outstanding; famous; easily seen
renowned (adj.) famous; celebrated; well-known; outstanding
sublime (adj.) marvelous; superb; great; awe-inspiring; splendid
ultimate (adj.) the greatest possible; supreme; final
vital (adj.) living; necessary to life; essential; important; lively; dynamic

Complete each sentence with the correct word from the box below.

barrage	compelled	monitor	novel	beseeched
confiscate	ration	renowned	allotted	prominent
reverberated	interminable	pivotal	crucial	prevalent
restricted				

1. The _____ decision to alter the ending of the novel was _____ to the completion of the book.

2. During the battle, the _____ of the cannons could be heard for miles.

3. It is vital to _____ a patient's life signs in the emergency room.

4. The singers' voices _____ throughout the concert hall.

5. It is the responsibility of the Border Patrol to search for illegal goods and _____ them.

6. The conductor _____ the audience to turn off their cell phones prior to the concert.

7. I thought the award ceremony was _____; it seemed as if the speakers went on for hours.

8. Each student was _____ two tickets for the music festival.

9. Someday I hope to challenge the _____ theory that life never existed on Mars.

10. His father is a(n) _____ physician in our town.

11. During the hurricane the town was _____ to _____ the water.

12. The area around the embassy was _____ to staff members only.

13. Her _____ haircut was imitated by all her friends.

14. The most _____ members of the community arrived at the banquet in limousines.

Match the word from Vocabulary List 15 (Column 1) with the correct definition (Column 2).

Column 1

_____ 1. interminable

_____ 2. prevalent

_____ 3. tumult

_____ 4. allot

_____ 5. compel

_____ 6. confiscate

_____ 7. dissuade

_____ 8. monitor

_____ 9. predominant

_____ 10. renowned

_____ 11. ultimate

_____ 12. ration

_____ 13. sublime

_____ 14. pinnacle

_____ 15. novel

_____ 16. vital

_____ 17. alter

_____ 18. beseech

Column 2

a. give little choice

b. racket

c. assign; dispense

d. innovative

e. greatest possible

f. oversee

g. plead with

h. famous

i. continuous

j. awe-inspiring

k. urge not to

l. revise

m. restrict amounts

n. commonly occurring

o. essential

p. zenith

q. important

r. impound

Complete the passage below using words from Vocabulary List 15.

A Compelling Talent

There is a(n) (1)_____ belief among most people, including renowned scientists and expert skateboarders, that human beings cannot safely float in the air for a(n) (2)_____ period of time without assistance. While curiosity might compel one to attempt this in the laboratory or on a sidewalk (with proper safety equipment, of course), a(n) (3)_____ and irksome problem is soon clear. Things—and people—fall. This vital fact tends to (4)_____ a repeat of the experiment.

However, one must consider the case of Mr. William X. As a prominent member of the community, he will remain unidentified. At the very (5)_____ of his career, when he was a predominant business, political, and social force, Mr. William X began to float in the air—all by himself. This was a(n) (6)_____ experience for his small town, but none attempted to (7)_____ his behavior. He was a generous man and tried to (8)_____ his floating time to all. Huge public demand, however, forced him to ration his floating time in one place. At town meetings, he spoke from the ceiling where his voice would (9)_____ throughout the hall, and he always received a(n) (10)_____ of cheers from both supporters and opponents. On the street, his performance was sublime, as his words carried above the (11)_____ of the crowds below to (12)_____ citizens to pay taxes, homeowners to (13)_____ pets, and drivers to slow down. One small drawback was a need for the local authorities to (14)_____ the size of crowds and confiscate the popular but dangerous plastic "Mr. William" wings.

His (15)_____ achievement was as a member of the community basketball team, where his defensive efforts against a team of visiting NBA stars were (16)_____ in the legendary upset victory. Unfortunately, since his feet never touched the ground, he never received an athletic shoe contract.

The heroes and heroines

These fearless champions are...

credible (adj.) reliable; dependable; conceivable; believable
ethical (adj.) moral; decent; virtuous; correct; honorable
forthright (adj.) frank; open; direct; candid
full of **integrity** (n.) honesty; principled; structural soundness; strength
just (adj.) fair; impartial; trustworthy; honest; moral; ethical
temperate (adj.) self-controlled; calm; level-headed; balmy; sunny
valiant (adj.) brave; courageous; heroic; intrepid; fearless; chivalrous
vigilant (adj.) watchful; attentive; careful; prudent
vulnerable (adj.) open to attack; weak; sensitive; defenseless; unprotected

Who seek...

an **alliance** (n.) agreement; pact; treaty; partnership; union
the **ideal** (adj.) having no flaw; perfect; standard of excellence; best situation
a **pact** (n.) treaty; agreement; alliance; understanding
a **quest** (n.) search; pursuit; mission; journey; adventure
a **truce** (n.) end to fighting; respite; pause; suspension of hostilities

What they do best

abstain (v.) hold back from doing something; avoid; refrain from
avert (v.) prevent; avoid; deter; turn away from; shift
confront (v.) stand up to; face boldly; challenge; oppose
empower (v.) give power to; permit; allow; authorize; sanction
endure (v.) put up with; withstand; tolerate; prevail; bear patiently; suffer
eradicate (v.) eliminate; destroy; expunge; abolish
foil (v.) keep from being successful; defeat; frustrate; thwart
intervene (v.) step in; mediate; intercede; take place
quell (v.) put an end to; conquer; defeat
repel (v.) drive back; rebuff; chase away; resist; disgust; nauseate
subdue (v.) overcome; conquer; calm; ease; soothe; relieve
vanquish (v.) defeat; win a victory; triumph over

Choose the correct definition for each word from Vocabulary List 16.

_____ 1. valiant
   a. having no flaw
   b. brave
   c. fair; impartial

_____ 2. quest
   a. search; pursuit
   b. curt; hold back
   c. a treaty

_____ 3. just
   a. defenseless; unprotected
   b. reliable
   c. fair; impartial

_____ 4. credible
   a. famous
   b. defeat
   c. reliable

_____ 5. subdue
   a. level-headed
   b. bear patiently
   c. overcome

_____ 6. truce
   a. pause; lull
   b. standard of excellence
   c. a favor

_____ 7. integrity
   a. honesty
   b. watchful
   c. believable

_____ 8. eradicate
   a. hold back; curb
   b. frank; open
   c. eliminate

_____ 9. vigilant
   a. decent
   b. frank; open
   c. watchful; careful

_____ 10. ideal
   a. level-headed
   b. having no flaw
   c. defeat

_____ 11. vulnerable
   a. defenseless; unprotected
   b. understanding
   c. give power to

_____ 12. pact
   a. assist
   b. frustrate
   c. a treaty

_____ 13. temperate
   a. turn away from
   b. face boldly
   c. calm; level-headed

_____ 14. ethical
   a. moral; decent
   b. frustrate
   c. weak

_____ 15. forthright
   a. search
   b. frank; open
   c. drive back

_____ 16. alliance
   a. reliable
   b. defeat
   c. agreement

Write Yes if the vocabulary word is used correctly and No if it is not.

_____ 1. A strike will **avert** trouble in the workplace.

_____ 2. Carnivores **abstain** from eating meat.

_____ 3. You should **confront** someone who wishes you well.

_____ 4. Music has been known to **quell** the fears of a frightened child.

_____ 5. A hiker needs **endurance** for a long trek in the wilderness.

_____ 6. After missing a meal you would be **repelled** by the mention of food.

_____ 7. Alert parents will **foil** their child's plot to stay up all night to watch videos.

_____ 8. It is wise to **intervene** in your friends' argument before emotions run too high.

_____ 9. A **credible** witness is one who cannot be trusted.

_____ 10. One would hope to choose friends who have **integrity**.

_____ 11. The **ideal** location for a home pool is in your front yard.

_____ 12. The promise of pizza has been known to **subdue** even the most famished of teens.

_____ 13. A **pact** between friends is a sure sign of the beginning of a fight.

_____ 14. A **truce** is the first step in cooling a feud.

_____ 15. A sensitive person is **vulnerable** to the cruel jokes of others.

Complete each sentence with the correct word from the box below.

empowered	alliance	vanquish	abstain	quest
quell	endure	confronting	just	forthright
foil	vigilant	avert	intervene	ideal
valiant				

1. The varsity team managed to _____ the state champions during the soccer tournament.

2. Sandbags were placed along the river's edge to _____ flooding.

3. The _____ knight rode off on his _____ in fulfillment of his vow.

4. Before _____ a problem, one must recognize it.

5. The policeman used his training to _____ the robbery.

6. Members of the United Nations supported the _____ between the hostile nations.

7. The _____ sentry remained alert through the severe storm.

8. My father is a(n) _____ person; he always listens to everyone's side of the story.

9. It is a challenge to _____ from playing those aggressive video games.

10. If you want a cat you must _____ its lofty personality as well as its amusing pranks.

11. The town's plan to _____ the plague of mosquitoes was not _____, but at least something was being done.

12. Managers do not always appreciate the _____ comments of other employees.

13. It is important to be cautious before you _____ between two fighting dogs.

14. Once you sign this application you will be _____ to open a credit card account.

The villains

Who they are

adversary (n.) rival; foe; antagonist; enemy; opponent
assailant (n.) one who attacks violently; attacker; aggressor
fanatic (n.) one who is overly enthusiastic about a belief; extremist; activist
menace (n.) danger; nuisance; threat
nemesis (n.) sworn enemy; rival; undoing; ruin; downfall
predator (n.) one who takes advantage of others; one who destroys for personal gain

Their actions are...

abominable (adj.) nasty; disgusting; very unpleasant; horrid
despicable (adj.) contemptible; completely unworthy of respect
dubious (adj.) questionable; suspicious; unreliable; skeptical
sinister (adj.) threatening; ominous; menacing; evil
subversive (adj.) treasonous; traitorous; undermining
treacherous (adj.) disloyal; deceitful; untrustworthy; unsafe; hazardous

Because they...

agitate (v.) stir up; upset; disturb; provoke; churn; excite
annihilate (v.) destroy completely; demolish; end; eradicate
besiege (v.) trouble with requests; pester; annoy; surround and attack
corrupt (v.) change from good to bad in morals or actions; lead astray; contaminate
hamper (v.) hold back; hinder; obstruct; inhibit
oppress (v.) tyrannize; keep someone down; weigh down with worry
snare (v.) trap; seize
stifle (v.) stop or hold back; unable to breathe freely; restrain
suppress (v.) put down by force; crush; keep secret; stop the publication of

And also...

bluff (v.) mislead; pretend; deceive; delude
conspire (v.) agree secretly to do an unlawful act; plot; scheme; connive
elude (v.) escape by being quick, skillful, or tricky; slip by
skulk (v.) move about in a sneaky way in order to remain unnoticed; slink

Solve the crossword puzzle below using words from Vocabulary List 17.

Across
1. trouble with requests
3. one who takes advantage of others
4. rival
7. keep someone down
8. disgusting
9. deceitful
11. trap
12. stir up
13. suspicious
14. hinder
15. danger

Down
2. put down by force
5. move about in a sneaky way
6. lead astray
8. one who attacks
10. scheme

Choose the correct word from Vocabulary List 17 for each item and circle it in the word search below.

C	E	P	R	E	D	A	T	O	R	Z	X	O	X	Q
I	O	L	U	K	S	L	Z	U	H	E	D	U	L	E
C	T	R	F	G	B	U	U	E	P	Z	J	E	S	R
U	K	N	R	I	D	L	L	H	S	L	M	U	Y	P
Z	N	H	L	U	T	E	K	J	T	D	D	S	I	J
V	D	X	D	I	P	S	S	N	J	R	R	B	S	R
R	J	F	Z	O	J	T	A	P	X	G	Z	J	C	A
H	R	F	F	D	J	L	E	A	I	Z	Q	J	U	T
K	Y	O	R	D	I	R	E	C	G	C	N	B	H	B
F	F	B	O	A	I	G	I	K	N	I	A	M	V	F
F	U	Q	S	P	E	T	B	I	C	I	T	B	F	S
U	U	S	S	I	A	H	M	V	S	S	X	A	L	T
L	A	N	S	N	Z	C	F	X	P	X	J	T	T	E
B	O	E	A	G	T	N	O	K	W	O	T	I	S	E
C	B	F	Q	N	N	N	A	N	Q	K	L	U	K	S

1. extremist

2. one who destroys for personal gain

3. attacker; aggressor

4. menacing; evil

5. unsafe; hazardous

6. deceive; pretend

7. surround and attack

8. provoke; excite

9. escape by being tricky

10. slink

11. plot; scheme

12. contaminate

13. stop or hold back

14. unworthy of respect

Choose the correct word for each item.

_____ 1. rival; foe

    a. subversive
    b. corrupter
    c. adversary

_____ 2. aggressor

    a. nemesis
    b. assailant
    c. fanatic

_____ 3. nuisance

    a. menace
    b. snare
    c. besiege

_____ 4. very unpleasant

    a. eradicate
    b. abominable
    c. predatory

_____ 5. completely unworthy of respect

    a. sinister
    b. despicable
    c. assailant

_____ 6. questionable

    a. dubious
    b. treacherous
    c. annihilate

_____ 7. threatening

    a. oppress
    b. vanquish
    c. sinister

_____ 8. untrustworthy; unsafe

    a. fanatical
    b. dubious
    c. treacherous

_____ 9. undermining

    a. suppress
    b. subversive
    c. stifle

_____ 10. destroy completely

    a. annihilate
    b. agitate
    c. vanquish

_____ 11. weigh down with worry

    a. bluff
    b. agitate
    c. oppress

_____ 12. trap

    a. nemesis
    b. snare
    c. hamper

_____ 13. restrain

    a. stifle
    b. fanatic
    c. conspire

_____ 14. plot; scheme

    a. assail
    b. hamper
    c. conspire

_____ 15. stop the publication of

    a. suppress
    b. agitate
    c. elude

_____ 16. obstruct; hinder

    a. elude
    b. hamper
    c. bluff

In the world of fantasy

Ogres can be...

colossal (adj.) immense; monstrous; huge; extraordinary; exceptional
grotesque (adj.) distorted; deformed; outlandish; absurd; bizarre; very odd
hideous (adj.) horribly ugly or disgusting; repulsive; appalling; loathsome
massive (adj.) immense; gigantic; monumental; heavy; weighty
putrid (adj.) rotten; foul-smelling; morally objectionable
vile (adj.) offensive; revolting; nasty; vulgar; morally bad; of little worth

They inhabit worlds that are...

barren (adj.) bare; desolate; producing little or no vegetation
bleak (adj.) desolate; gloomy; dismal; grim; forbidding
desolate (adj.) deserted; without signs of life; filled with sorrow; abandoned
eerie (adj.) strange; mysterious; weird; inspiring fear; frightening; uneasy
enchanted (adj.) bewitched; charmed; mesmerized
murky (adj.) dark; gloomy; misty; foggy; dreary; somber
ominous (adj.) threatening; menacing; foreboding; sinister

Tricksters are...

cunning (adj.) foxy; wily; sly; deceptive; deceitful; devious
shrewd (adj.) sly; crafty; tricky; shifty; astute; clever; sharp-witted
stealthy (adj.) underhanded; sneaky; sly; devious; secretive
tantalizing (adj.) teasing; tempting; provoking
wily (adj.) clever in a sneaky and tricky way; calculating; shrewd

Because they...

bewilder (v.) perplex; confuse; puzzle completely; baffle; mystify
conjure (v.) make appear; call forth by magical words; practice magic
deceive (v.) mislead; cheat; swindle
distort (v.) deform; misshape; misrepresent; twist the meaning of
feign (v.) pretend; fake; simulate; make up; forge
mimic (v.) imitate; make fun of; parrot; impersonate
plague (v.) torment; perturb; harass; bother

Complete each sentence with the correct word from the box below.

bewildered	murky	mimicked	massive	wily
ominous	bleak	putrid	conjured	desolate
tantalizing	cunning	grotesque	distort	vile
stealthy	eerie	hideous	shrewd	

1. The _____, barren, and _____ island had a(n) _____ affect on the settlers.

2. The author _____ in his mind a(n) _____ and _____ character for the villainous role in his novel.

3. In the African jungles, tigers often make a(n) _____ descent upon villages, killing hundreds.

4. A food critic reviewed the newest restaurant: "Two thumbs down. The food at that restaurant can only be rated as _____ and _____."

5. The water at the shore's edge was _____ and still, but farther out it became clear and _____ to the divers.

6. The _____ and _____ fox clearly outwitted the hounds and escaped.

7. The construction of the dam will be a(n) _____ achievement when completed.

8. The ape _____ his caretaker's every move and then laughed.

9. The fishermen observed _____ clouds on the horizon.

10. The hikers were _____ as to which trail they should take back to camp.

11. The banker was a(n) _____ businessman; he was known for the clever ways he handled his business ventures.

12. Scratched glasses will _____ your vision.

Use words from Vocabulary List 18 to find the hidden message.

"What do you call a tricky imposter?"

1. __ __ ◯ ◯ __ __ __ __   confuse; perplex

2. ◯ __ __ __ __ ◯ __   misrepresent

3. __ ◯ __ __ __   pretend, fake

4. __ __ __ ◯ __ __   crafty; shifty; clever

5. ◯ __ __ ◯ __   revolting

6. __ __ __ __ ◯ __ __ ◯   underhanded; devious

7. ◯ __ __ __ ◯ __ __   sly; deceptive

Hidden Message: "A __ __ __ __   __ __ __ __ __ __ __ __ "
                 1   1   6   6   2   3   7   4   7   5   5   2

Match the definition in Column 1 to the correct word from Vocabulary List 18 in Column 2.

Column 1

_____ 1. vulgar; morally bad

_____ 2. fascinated; charmed

_____ 3. horribly ugly

_____ 4. rotten; foul-smelling

_____ 5. strange; mysterious

_____ 6. imitate

_____ 7. clever in a sneaky way

_____ 8. teasing; tempting

_____ 9. distorted; deformed

_____ 10. threatening; sinister

_____ 11. dark; gloomy

_____ 12. dismal; grim; forbidding

_____ 13. cheat; swindle

_____ 14. immense; extraordinary

_____ 15. gigantic; heavy

_____ 16. twist the meaning of

_____ 17. produce no vegetation

_____ 18. make appear

_____ 19. pretend; fake

_____ 20. torment

Column 2

a. colossal

b. grotesque

c. conjure

d. ominous

e. vile

f. feign

g. massive

h. eerie

i. hideous

j. enchanted

k. plague

l. wily

m. deceive

n. bleak

o. mimic

p. barren

q. tantalizing

r. distort

s. putrid

t. murky

Choose the correct synonym and antonym for each word from Vocabulary Lists 15–18.

POWer Word	S	A	Synonym	Antonym
1. credible	____	____	A. respite	a. corrupt
2. just	____	____	B. put up with	b. calm down
3. vigilant	____	____	C. tremendous	c. clean
4. truce	____	____	D. believable	d. warfare
5. temperate	____	____	E. unproductive	e. encourage
6. vanquish	____	____	F. deny oneself	f. comforting
7. endure	____	____	G. competitor	g. fight against
8. abstain	____	____	H. creepy	h. confront
9. adversary	____	____	I. fair-minded	i. unbelievable
10. sinister	____	____	J. avoid	j. clear
11. stifle	____	____	K. evil	k. excitable
12. elude	____	____	L. gloomy	l. productive
13. colossal	____	____	M. on guard	m. inattentive
14. barren	____	____	N. suppress	n. obvious
15. eerie	____	____	O. provoke	o. teammate
16. murky	____	____	P. overpower	p. surrender
17. hideous	____	____	Q. ugly	q. little
18. putrid	____	____	R. rancid	r. attractive
19. stealthy	____	____	S. level-headed	s. honorable
20. agitate	____	____	T. sneaky	t. self-indulgent

Complete the charts with the correct words from the box below.

irksome	empower	alliance	deceive	foil
beseech	corrupt	bluff	forthright	predators
quest	alter	oppress	agitate	fanatical
pivotal	dissuade	conspire	crucial	adversarial
intervene	despicable	temperate	compelling	

My Hero

Who or What He Is

1. _____
2. _____
3. _____
4. _____
5. _____

His Goal

1. _____
   _____
2. _____
   _____

How He'll Get It

1. _____
2. _____
3. _____
4. _____
5. _____

The Nasty Villain

Who or What He Is

1. _____
2. _____
3. _____
4. _____
5. _____

His Goal

1. _____
   _____
2. _____
   _____

How He'll Get It

1. _____
2. _____
3. _____
4. _____
5. _____

Circle the word that does NOT belong in each set.

1. barrage   stifle   reverberation   tumult

2. interminable restrict   hamper   dissuade

3. plague   suppress   repel   endure

4. ethical   abominable   just   forthright

5. renowned   valiant   dubious   prominent

6. bluff   skulk   feign   enchanted

7. sinister   treacherous   prevalent   despicable

8. vanquish   confiscate   snare   conspire

9. pinnacle   sublime   ultimate   subversive

10. pivotal   bleak   vital   crucial

POWer Maze

Directions: Find your way out of the maze. Begin at START. Move up, down, left, right, or diagonally. Clues for each move are listed below.

putrid	nemesis	feign	murky	pivotal	**EXIT?**	quell
defect	colossal	wily	cunning	defect	crucial	colossal
prominent	quell	predator	stifle	skulk	cunning	massive
EXIT?	alliance	integrity	repel	compel	shrewd	colossal
pivotal	massive	pact	ration	beseech	quell	crucial
conjure	entreat	prominent	vital	renowned	predominant	**EXIT?**

START

Clues

1. necessary to life
2. famous
3. beg
4. require
5. restrict amount
6. an agreement
7. honesty
8. partnership
9. one who takes advantage of others
10. stop; hold back
11. move about in a sneaky way
12. sly; tricky; crafty
13. gloomy
14. fake
15. calculating
16. huge
17. put an end to
18. important

Tricky words

access (n.) admittance; entrance; entry
excess (n.) surplus; overabundance; profusion

affect (v.) influence; change; modify; have an emotional effect on
effect (n.) result; consequence; outcome; upshot

allusion (n.) reference made to something that is not directly mentioned; hint
illusion (n.) misleading visual impression; delusion; deception

cede (v.) hand over; surrender; give; relinquish
secede (v.) withdraw; leave; quit

confidant (n.) a person to whom secrets are entrusted; close friend
confident (adj.) self-assured; self-sufficient; certain; sure; positive

council (n.) an advisory or legislative body; committee
counsel (n.) advice given from a trusted person; exchange of opinions; legal advisor

hoard (v.) store up; save; amass
horde (n.) a large crowd; a vast number of people; a throng; multitude

idle (adj.) out of work; not being used; lazy; sluggish; worthless; pointless
idol (n.) a popular hero; public favorite; an image worshiped as a god

momentous (adj.) very important; crucial; significant; serious
momentum (n.) the force of speed with which something moves; drive; thrust

persecute (v.) annoy cruelly; pester; cause to suffer; torment
prosecute (v.) put on trial; indict; take legal action; arraign

principal (adj.) most important; leading; dominant; first; head of a school
principle (n.) truth; regulation; belief; attitude; morality; standards; rule of conduct

punctilious (adj.) exact; precise; correct; exacting; strict; fussy
punctual (adj.) prompt; on time; immediate

Choose the correct word from Vocabulary List 19 for each item.

_____ 1. hint

    a. confidant

    b. illusion

    c. allusion

_____ 2. surplus

    a. hoard

    b. access

    c. excess

_____ 3. hand over

    a. punctual

    b. secede

    c. cede

_____ 4. change; modify

    a. idol

    b. effect

    c. affect

_____ 5. deception

    a. allusion

    b. illusion

    c. access

_____ 6. a large crowd

    a. council

    b. hoard

    c. horde

_____ 7. entrance

    a. access

    b. counsel

    c. punctual

_____ 8. close friend

    a. idol

    b. confidant

    c. confident

_____ 9. take legal action

    a. punctilious

    b. persecute

    c. prosecute

_____10. withdraw

    a. secede

    b. confident

    c. momentum

_____11. annoy cruelly

    a. persecute

    b. punctual

    c. prosecute

_____12. advice given

    a. principal

    b. counsel

    c. affect

_____13. force of speed

    a. idle

    b. momentum

    c. momentous

_____14. consequence; result

    a. effect

    b. affect

    c. cede

_____15. an advisory committee

    a. council

    b. principle

    c. principal

_____16. self-assured

    a. hoard

    b. punctilious

    c. confident

Complete each sentence with the correct word from the box below.

punctilious	idle	idol	prosecuted	hordes
affect	allusion	ceded	principal	momentous
persecuted	momentum	excessive	punctuality	hoard
principles				

1. When Dad's company downsized, he was _____ for three months before receiving a new job offer.

2. The Pilgrims came to the New World after being _____ for their religious _____.

3. Normally Al was _____ in checking his bank statement, but lately his approach has been more haphazard.

4. Once the castle's defenses were breached, angry _____ climbed over the walls.

5. I have never ridden a roller coaster; its _____ frightens me.

6. Today's paper announced that my baseball _____ would be visiting the mall.

7. The speeder was _____ for his rash behavior.

8. My sister announced that she was chosen to be the _____ soloist in the spring play.

9. We all know people who are so obsessed with _____ that their habit becomes annoying.

10. Before Grandma moved to a smaller apartment, she would _____ newspapers in her dining room.

11. The blizzard will not _____ our plans to go skiing.

12. It will be a(n) _____ occasion when our misbehaving puppy finally becomes trained.

13. It is quite easy to drink a(n) _____ amount of soda.

14. In her closing remarks, the prime minister made a brief _____ to earlier trade agreement failures.

15. The Utah Territory was _____ to the United States by Mexico in 1848.

Choose the correct word from Vocabulary List 19 for each item and circle it in the word search below.

D	H	H	X	W	M	E	Y	D	C	Q	T	A	Q	Q
A	C	O	A	B	F	G	E	Q	S	N	C	X	U	Z
M	K	O	A	Z	Z	A	A	Z	E	C	Z	P	Y	A
M	Z	D	N	R	Q	A	O	D	E	T	S	I	A	E
O	E	N	Z	F	D	Z	I	S	R	Z	S	J	J	N
Y	G	I	R	M	I	F	S	K	L	G	N	V	K	I
V	S	Y	B	M	N	D	I	T	U	Q	F	H	G	R
L	C	T	K	O	E	R	A	L	T	D	T	N	Y	X
Q	Z	C	C	D	K	W	W	N	L	C	U	K	D	J
C	I	Q	E	Y	K	B	S	L	T	U	E	Y	R	I
I	G	C	W	L	R	G	O	S	K	V	S	F	H	F
G	E	W	Y	B	N	G	P	P	O	U	F	I	F	X
S	I	D	L	E	Y	X	T	T	B	D	K	W	O	E
D	U	V	U	Y	M	P	L	E	S	N	U	O	C	N
D	K	T	P	G	O	C	O	L	I	C	N	U	O	C

1. entry
2. outcome
3. misleading visual impression
4. withdraw
5. close friend
6. committee
7. advice
8. self-assured
9. store up
10. lazy

More tricky words

abate (v.) reduce; decrease; diminish; ease; relieve; alleviate
abet (v.) encourage; support; uphold; urge; incite; aid

accept (v.) receive or take willingly; agree to; assume; admit
except (v.) exempt; excuse; exclude; ban; shut out

adapt (v.) adjust; confirm; accommodate; rework
adept (adj.) highly skilled; expert; very good at something

complement (n.) supplement; completion; full amount; necessary amount
compliment (n.) an admiring remark; sincere praise; adulation

discreet (v.) careful not to reveal too much; tactful; diplomatic
discrete (v.) separate; distinct; independent

flammable (adj.) capable of being easily set on fire and of burning rapidly
inflammable (adj.) easily set on fire; easily angered; excitable

flout (v.) show contempt for; laugh at; mock
flaunt (v.) display in a conceited way; show off; advertise; brag; flourish; wave

hurdle (n.) obstacle; difficulty; problem; barrier to be jumped in a race
hurtle (v.) move with great force and speed; rush; dash

incredible (adj.) unbelievable; remarkable; inconceivable; astounding
incredulous (adj.) unwilling or unable to believe; skeptical; doubtful

infer (v.) arrive at as a conclusion; guess; speculate; surmise
imply (v.) suggest rather than say plainly; hint; presume

prescribe (v.) recommend; stipulate; order; establish; authorize
proscribe (v.) outlaw; prohibit; denounce; disapprove; ban

prior (adj.) previous; preexisting; earlier
priority (n.) greater; preference; urgency

Complete each sentence by circling the correct word.

1. It is an (accepted, excepted) fact that continuous high winds will damage the shoreline.

2. When our family moved south we had to (adept, adapt) to winters without snow.

3. I sold my old computer along with its (complement, compliment) of software.

4. I was able to discover his birthday by asking (discreet, discrete) questions of his sister.

5. Her (flammable, inflammable) personality made smooth friendships impossible.

6. We all appreciate (complements, compliments).

7. She (flaunted, flouted) her parents' rules by going to the mall.

8. I put everything (except, accept) my videos on a shelf.

9. Don't (imply, infer) that I dislike rap just because I am picky when choosing a radio station.

10. My little brother was aided and (abetted, abated) by the family pooch when he ran off with all the cookies.

11. The young chess player demonstrated (incredulous, incredible) patience as he waited for his opponent to make a move.

12. The runners (hurdled, hurtled) down the track as the starter's whistle blew.

13. I wanted to go to the party, but I had a (prior, priority) engagement.

Match the word from Vocabulary List 20 (Column 1) with the correct definition (Column 2).

Column 1

_____ 1. hurtle

_____ 2. inflammable

_____ 3. abate

_____ 4. hurdle

_____ 5. infer

_____ 6. abet

_____ 7. accept

_____ 8. flammable

_____ 9. priority

_____ 10. imply

_____ 11. prescribe

_____ 12. adept

_____ 13. proscribe

_____ 14. incredible

_____ 15. flout

_____ 16. compliment

_____ 17. except

_____ 18. adapt

_____ 19. flaunt

_____ 20. incredulous

_____ 21. complement

_____ 22. discreet

_____ 23. discrete

_____ 24. prior

Column 2

a. show off

b. unbelievable

c. exclude; shut out

d. encourage; support

e. adjust; rework

f. previous; preexisting

g. full amount; supplement

h. unwilling to believe; skeptical

i. separate; distinct

j. agree to; take willingly

k. careful not to reveal too much

l. easily set on fire

m. expert

n. reduce; decrease

o. show contempt for; laugh at

p. recommend; establish

q. suggest rather than say plainly

r. an admiring remark

s. ban; prohibit

t. easily angered; excitable

u. preference; urgency

v. move with great force and speed

w. arrive at a conclusion

x. obstacle; difficulty

Answer each of the following questions.

_____ 1. Would first-aid cream help to **abet** your sunburn?

_____ 2. Would you be **flaunting** the school dress code rules if you wore a shirt and tie to school?

_____ 3. Would you be able to jump a **hurtle** placed three inches off the ground?

_____ 4. Should you be **discreet** when answering personal questions?

_____ 5. Would a veterinarian **proscribe** medicine for your ill pet?

_____ 6. If you wanted someone to receive your letter quickly should you send it by **prior** mail?

_____ 7. Are there **prescribed** rules of etiquette for eating in a restaurant?

_____ 8. Are **flammable** pajamas the safest for children?

_____ 9. Would it be **incredible** if an adult believed in the Tooth Fairy?

_____ 10. Should an active social life be your first **priority** in school?

_____ 11. Should a surfer be **adept** at maintaining his/her balance before seeking the monster wave?

_____ 12. Should you **complement** your mother after a tasty meal?

_____ 13. Is it possible to **adapt** to living in a cold climate?

_____ 14. Would it be appropriate to invite all your classmates **except** one to a party?

_____ 15. Do you think some students consider math an impossible **hurdle** to overcome?

_____ 16. Do people who refuse to pay parking tickets **flout** the law?

Use words from Vocabulary Lists 19–20 to find the hidden message.

"Why can't the detective put his son's bicycle together?"

1. ___ ___ ___ ◯   a popular hero

2. ___ ___ ___ ___ ___ ___ ___ ___ ___ ◯   belief

3. ___ ___ ___ ___ ___ ___ ___ ___ ___ ◯   significant

4. ___ ___ ◯ ___ ___ ___ ___ ___   separate; distinct

5. ___ ___ ___ ◯ ___   suggest rather than say

6. ___ ___ ___ ___ ___ ◯ ___ ___   prompt

7. ___ ___ ___ ◯ ___   speculate

8. ___ ___ ___ ___ ___ ◯ ___ ___ ___   torment

9. ◯ ___ ___ ___   not being used

10. ___ ___ ___ ◯ ___   surplus

Hidden Message: "He ___ ___ ___ ___ ___ ___ ___ ___ ___ ___."
9 4   8 1 6 2 5 7 3 10

Choose the correct definition for each word from Vocabulary Lists 19–20.

_____ 1. affect

    a. leave

    b. outcome

    c. have an emotional effect on

_____ 2. allusion

    a. hint

    b. exact

    c. deception

_____ 3. cede

    a. leave

    b. modify

    c. hand over

_____ 4. confident

    a. arraign

    b. positive of

    c. close friend

_____ 5. council

    a. guidance

    b. crucial

    c. committee

_____ 6. horde

    a. multitude

    b. annoy cruelly

    c. store up

_____ 7. prosecute

    a. pester

    b. prompt

    c. take legal action

_____ 8. punctilious

    a. on time

    b. certain

    c. exacting; fussy

_____ 9. abate

    a. a throng

    b. incite

    c. relieve

_____ 10. flout

    a. mock

    b. brag

    c. presume

_____ 11. hurdle

    a. remarkable

    b. rush

    c. problem

_____ 12. incredulous

    a. skeptical

    b. previous

    c. remarkable

_____ 13. prior

    a. earlier

    b. independent

    c. preference

_____ 14. proscribe

    a. order

    b. prohibit

    c. excuse

_____ 15. discrete

    a. separate

    b. careful not to reveal too much

    c. outlaw

_____ 16. incredible

    a. suggest

    b. inconceivable

    c. confirm

Complete each of the following with a word from Vocabulary Lists 11–20.

1. __ __ __ __ K Y   having an odd personal habit

2. __ __ H I __ __ __   virtuous; honorable

3. __ __ __ A K   dismal; grim

4. __ U T __ __ __   rotten; foul-smelling

5. __ __ __ O R __   mutual understanding

6. __ __ N Y   nonsensical; inane

7. M A __ __ __ __   gigantic; monumental

8. __ I L __   nasty; vulgar

9. __ __ __ P A __ __ __ __ __   empathy; mercy

10. __ __ __ __ __ __ __ C A __   shared; mutual

11. __ L A __ __ __ __ __ __   one who makes false statements

12. __ __ I D   have a strong desire for

13. __ A R __ __ __ __   noise

14. __ V A __ __ __ __   greed

15. __ __ __ __ __ __ __ N E   intercede; mediate

16. __ __ W I __ __ __ __   baffle; confuse

Word Board Challenger

CLUES: definition, the list where the word is found, and the number of letters in the word; For example, the answer to Clue #1 (escalate) is found in Vocabulary List 11 and has eight letters.

DIRECTIONS:
1. Player #1 writes the answer to a clue anywhere on the Word Board (see p. 117). Do not use a square with a value of 10 for the first move.
2. Each player in turn selects a clue and writes its POWer Word on the Word Board. All words must link crossword style.
3. Clues may be used only once and need not be solved in order. Not all clues will be used in every game.
4. Game is over once all clues, or as many as possible, are played.

SCORING: Players add up their scores. All values of letters, even those previously played, count. Winner has most points.

CLUES

1. increase in intensity (List #11; 8)
2. brag (List #12; 5)
3. wonder (List #13; 3)
4. bother (List #18; 6)
5. do a favor for (List #14; 6)
6. abandoned (List #18; 8)
7. tendency (List #11; 11)
8. impartial (List #16; 4)
9. tactful (List #20; 8)
10. flinch (List #13; 6)
11. suggest rather than say (List #20; 5)
12. distribute (List #15; 5)
13. rule of conduct (List #19; 9)
14. nonsensical (List #11; 4)
15. put an end to (List #16; 5)
16. struck with horror and dismay (List #13; 6)
17. popular hero (List #19; 4)
18. modify (List #15; 5)
19. a deceiver (List #12; 11)
20. belittle (List #12; 5)
21. one who pries (List #12; 7)
22. deceive (List #17; 5)
23. idea (List #14; 6)
24. sworn enemy (List #17; 7)
25. towering (List #12; 5)
26. freedom from punishment (List #14; 8)

Word Board

5					3		3					5
	4		10							10	4	
		3				4				3		
			2			1			2			
				1	4		4	1				
	10										10	
2					3	5	3					2
		5				1				5		
				1	10			1				
			2					10	2			
		3				4				3		
	4		10							10		4
5					4			4				5

NOTE: The number in the square represents the value (number of points) of the letter written on that square.

Choose the correct definition for each word from Vocabulary Lists 11–20.

_____ 1. proficient

    a. masterful

    b. phony

    c. bothersome

_____ 2. delude

    a. give no chance

    b. watch dog

    c. con

_____ 3. gloat

    a. rejoice selfishly

    b. odd-shaped

    c. picky

_____ 4. predominant

    a. show disbelief

    b. second to none

    c. heckle

_____ 5. aghast

    a. turn one's back on

    b. thunderstruck

    c. celebrity

_____ 6. berate

    a. bawl out

    b. forsake

    c. cause for alarm

_____ 7. cringe

    a. nip

    b. baffle

    c. flinch

_____ 8. wretched

    a. tiff

    b. insubordinate

    c. sick at heart

_____ 9. revelation

    a. eye opener

    b. loathe

    c. ill-starred

_____ 10. perspective

    a. odd-shaped

    b. convey

    c. bird's-eye view

_____ 11. vanquish

    a. reverberate

    b. get the upper hand over

    c. show disbelief

_____ 12. fanatic

    a. squeal

    b. hot head

    c. abate

_____ 13. bluff

    a. adversary

    b. pinnacle

    c. bamboozle

_____ 14. mimic

    a. parrot

    b. crucial

    c. subdue

_____ 15. punctilious

    a. picky

    b. give out

    c. tantalizing

_____ 16. abet

    a. avert

    b. once and for all

    c. egg on

Solve the crossword puzzle below using words from Vocabulary Lists 1–20.

Across
2. very unpleasant
3. shade of meaning
6. unsafe
7. without end
9. catastrophe
13. approval
17. symbolic story
18. consider; reveal
19. move quickly

Down
1. crisis; predicament
2. absence of government
4. being in danger of injury
5. attacker
8. symbol whose value can change
10. full of detail
11. ample; huge
12. a preserve
14. gather
15. distorted; difficult to understand
16. trouble with requests

Use words from Vocabulary Lists 1–20 to find the hidden message.

1. __ __ __ __ ⭕   hint

2. __ __ __ __ ⭕ __ __   suspicious; skeptical

3. __ __ ⭕ __ __   a stop in fighting

4. __ __ __ ⭕ __   grim; dismal

5. __ __ __ ⭕ __ __   lead astray

6. __ ⭕ __ __ __   frightening; weird

7. __ __ ⭕ __ __   trap

8. __ __ __ ⭕ __ __ __ __   tactful; diplomatic

9. __ __ ⭕ __ __ __   torment; bother

10. __ __ ⭕ __ __ __ __   oversee

11. __ __ ⭕ __ __ __   bear patiently

12. __ __ __ ⭕ __ __ __   crucial; vital

13. __ __ __ ⭕ __   very good at something

14. __ __ ⭕ __ __   journey

15. __ __ __ ⭕ __ __   desolate

16. __ __ __ ⭕ __ __ __   annoying

17. __ ⭕ __ __ __   store up; save

18. __ __ __ ⭕ __ __ __   legal advisor

Hidden Message: "__ __ __ __ __ __ __ ' __ __ __ __ __"
              1   2   3   4   5   6   7   8   9   10   11   12

__ __ __ __ __ __."
13   14   15   16   17   18

Choose the correct word from Vocabulary Lists 1–20 for each item.

1. m e __ __ __ __   nuisance; threat

2. m e __ __ __ __ __   one who pries

3. m e __ __ __ __ __ __ __   erratic; fickle

4. m e __ __ __ __   spirit; determination

5. __ m e __ __   fix

6. __ __ m e __ __ __   sworn enemy

7. __ __ m e __ __ __ __   speed; drive

8. __ __ m e __ __ __ __ __   crucial; significant

9. __ __ __ m e __ __ __ __ __ __   being at fault

10. __ __ __ m e __ __ __   start

11. __ __ __ m e   first in importance

12. __ __ __ __ m e __ __ __   outer edge

13. __ __ __ __ __ m e   awe-inspiring; splendid

14. __ __ __ __ __ m e   annoying

15. __ __ __ __ __ m e __ __ __   rarity; marvel

16. __ __ __ __ __ __ m e __ __   full amount

17. __ __ __ __ __ __ m e __ __   sincere praise

18. __ __ __ __ __ __ m e __ __   outcome

Answer each of the following questions.

Who would...

1. lie under oath?

    nomad   buffoon   perjurer

2. risk starting a new business?

    tyrant   entrepreneur   embezzler

3. pretend to be your friend?

    braggart   bigot   hypocrite

4. interrupt when you are chatting with your friends?

    meddlers   slanderers   manipulators

5. boast about the amount of high marks received?

    inhibitors   species   braggarts

6. leave his country to live elsewhere?

    nomad   immigrant   buffoon

7. instigate an argument?

    slanderer   nomad   aggressor

8. attempt to rescue a cat?

    the just   the repulsive   the valiant

9. call for the closing of all hamburger restaurants due to a belief in vegetarian meals only?

    bigots   fanatics   optimists

10. believe themselves to be superior to everyone else?

    the obstinate   the forlorn   the elite

Match the word from Vocabulary Lists 1–20 (Column 1) with the correct definition (Column 2).

Column 1

_____ 1. inflammable

_____ 2. confidant

_____ 3. tantalizing

_____ 4. enchanted

_____ 5. skulk

_____ 6. elude

_____ 7. conspire

_____ 8. besiege

_____ 9. dubious

_____ 10. pinnacle

_____ 11. novel

_____ 12. curt

_____ 13. discretion

_____ 14. quench

_____ 15. ornate

_____ 16. exquisite

_____ 17. saunter

_____ 18. frank

_____ 19. instill

_____ 20. perpendicular

_____ 21. myth

_____ 22. incoherent

Column 2

a. a story of gods

b. superb

c. good judgment

d. impart; inspire

e. move about in a sneaky way

f. highest point of achievement

g. plot; scheme

h. questionable

i. walk in a casual way

j. close friend

k. blunt

l. easily set on fire

m. outspoken; honest

n. a line at right angles

o. charmed

p. surround and attack

q. tempting; provoking

r. elaborately decorated

s. unclear in speech

t. escape by being skillful

u. original; innovative

v. bring to an end

Complete each sentence with the correct words.

_____ 1. A grandparent's _____ joy is when the grandkids ask for advice on _____ decisions.

    (a) despicable…crucial   (b) predominant…controversial   (c) ultimate…momentous
    (d) irksome…vital   (e) pivotal…concurring

_____ 2. Although Mark appears to be _____, those who know him appreciate his _____ nature.

    (a) sinister…fluctuating   (b) tolerant…bellowing   (c) principled…incredible
    (d) obstinate…enthusiastic   (e) swaggering…unscrupulous

_____ 3. Some political cartoons are designed to _____ the reader, others to show the artist's _____.

    (a) compel…apprehension   (b) enlighten…disdain   (c) vindicate…ideals
    (d) astonish…barrage   (e) oppress…empowerment

_____ 4. The _____ tone of the news article further aggravated the already _____ conditions on the island.

    (a) subversive…turbulent   (b) distorted…enchanted   (c) hideous…jovial
    (d) prior…flammable   (e) accomplished…pinnacle

_____ 5. We _____ situations in which new students are _____.

    (a) forsake…transformed   (b) rectify…acknowledged   (c) solicit…vulnerable
    (d) prosecute…forthright   (e) deplore…ostracized

_____ 6. It is _____ to avoid _____ those with whom you disagree.

    (a) prevalent…dissuading   (b) unique…agitating   (c) crucial…harassing
    (d) impunity…relinquishing   (e) quirk…gratifying

_____ 7. She used to be _____ to my suggestions, but her recent hesitation _____ me.

    (a) wistful…corrupts   (b) nuance…suppresses   (c) restricted…foils
    (d) receptive…baffles   (e) puncture…illusions

_____ 8. I have to _____ the fact that my younger sister will _____ her candy instead of sharing.

    (a) marvel…compromise   (b) contemplate…terminate   (c) impose…detest
    (d) repel…realm   (e) accept…hoard

Index
of
POWer Words

Notes

 ⋯ *POWer Words™ Grades 7–8*

A

abate 20
abdicate 5
abet 20
abominable 17
abrupt 7
abstain 16
absurd 8
accept 20
access 19
accommodate 1
accomplish 10
accord 11
accumulate 8
acknowledge 14
acquire 8
adapt 20
adept 20
adequate 6
adjacent 4
adversary 17
advice 14
affect 19
affirmation 6
agenda 5
aggression 14
aghast 13
agitate 17
allegation 14
allegiance 5
allegory 4
alliance 16
allot 15
allusion 19
alter 15
altercation 14
alternative 10
amble 8
amend 5
analogy 4
analyze 3
anarchy 5
anecdote 4
annex 5

annihilate 17
anticipate 1
apprehension 13
apprentice 5
approximate 4
arid 3
assailant 17
assent 6
assert 1
assimilate 1
astonish 7
astronomy 3
asylum 6
avarice 14
avert 16
avid 13
awe 13

B

baffle 11
barrage 15
barren 18
bellow 7
berate 13
beseech 15
besiege 17
bestow 8
bewilder 18
bias 5
bigot 12
blameworthy 12
bleak 18
bluff 17
blunder 9
boisterous 1
bolster 10
botch 9
boycott 5
braggart 11
brood 13
buffoon 11
buoyant 1

C

calamity 6
capacious 6
cede 19
celestial 3
chafe 13
chaos 6
clamor 7
clarify 10
cliché 2
collaborate 2
colossal 18
commence 10
compassion 11
compel 15
competent 1
complement 20
compliment 20
compromise 7
concur 7
confidant 19
confident 19
confiscate 15
confront 16
conjecture 3
conjure 18
connotation 4
consolidate 5
conspire 17
contemplate 10
controversy 14
conventional 8
convey 14
cope 2
corrupt 17
council 19
counsel 19
cower 13
cram 2
credible 16
cringe 13
crucial 15
cunning 18
curt 12

D

deceive 18
decree 5
defect 5
delectable 8
delude 11
denouement 4
deplore 13
deprive 11
desolate 18
despair 13
despicable 17
despondent 13
detest 13
dexterous 9
diminish 11
discern 14
discourse 14
discreet 20
discrete 20
discretion 11
disdain 13
disposition 11
dissuade 15
distort 18
diversity 5
divert 14
divulge 7
dogged 1
drab 6
dubious 17

E

eclipse 3
eerie 18
effect 19
elated 1
elite 12
eloquent 1
elude 17
embargo 5
embezzler 12
empathy 11
empower 16
enchanted 18
endeavor 10

endure 16
enlighten 14
enthusiasm 10
entice 8
entreat 7
entrepreneur 5
eradicate 16
escalate 11
estimate 4
ethical 16
evolve 3
exasperating 7
except 20
excess 19
exhausting 7
exhilaration 10
expenditure 5
exquisite 8
extraordinary 7
exuberant 13

F

fallacy 14
fanatic 17
feign 18
feint 9
fervent 9
feud 14
flammable 20
flaunt 20
flourish 9
flout 20
fluctuate 11
flustered 1
foil 16
folly 6
forfeit 9
forlorn 13
forsake 11
forthright 16
foster 7
frank 7
frenzied 9
friction 3
frivolous 8
fusion 3

G

garbled 2
genial 1
gloat 12
grapple 2
gratify 8
gravity 3
grotesque 18

H

haggle 8
hamper 17
haphazard 9
harass 13
hideous 18
hoard 19
horde 19
humdrum 2
hurdle 20
hurtle 20
hypocrite 12
hypothesis 3

I

ideal 16
idle 19
idol 19
illegible 2
illiterate 2
illusion 19
immaculate 6
immigrant 5
imperious 12
implore 7
imply 20
impose 7
impudent 12
impunity 14
incentive 5
incoherent 2
incomprehensible 2
incredible 20
incredulous 20
indefinite 2
indignation 13

inept 9
inert 3
infer 20
infinite 4
inflammable 20
infuriate 13
inhibited 1
inquisitive 2
insinuation 14
inspiration 10
instill 7
insubordinate 12
integrity 16
interminable 15
intervene 16
intricate 9
invincible 10
irksome 15
irrelevant 2

J
jar 10
jeopardy 6
jovial 1
jumble 6
just 16

K
keen 1

L
labyrinth 6
lavish 8
legacy 5
linger 10
literal 4
lithe 9
loaf 8
loathe 13
lofty 12
lustrous 8

M
maneuver 9
manipulator 12
marvel 6
massive 18
maze 6
meddler 12
menace 17
mercurial 11
mettle 1
mimic 18
mingle 1
momentous 19
momentum 19
monitor 15
monotonous 2
motivated 1
murky 18
muse 10
myth 4

N
nemesis 17
nimble 9
nomad 5
notion 14
novel 15
nuance 4
nucleus 3

O
oblige 14
oblivious 1
obstinate 12
ominous 18
oppress 17
optimist 10
orbit 3
organism 3
ornate 8
ostracize 12
overbearing 11

P
pact 16
painstaking 9
palpable 3
parable 4
paradox 4
peculiar 1
perceive 2
peril 6
perimeter 4
perjurer 12
perpendicular 4
perplexed 1
persecute 19
persevere 2
persistent 2
perspective 14
persuade 7
phenomenon 3
pinnacle 15
pivotal 15
plague 18
plight 6
ponder 2
porous 3
precise 9
predator 17
predict 3
predominant 15
prescribe 20
prevail 9
prevalent 15
prime 4
principal 19
principle 19
prior 20
priority 20
probe 7
proficient 11
prominent 15
proscribe 20
prosecute 19
proximity 11
pseudonym 4
pun 4
punctilious 19

punctual 19
pungent 8
putrid 18

Q

quell 16
quench 8
query 2
quest 16
quibble 7
quirky 11

R

rambling 2
random 4
rankle 13
ratify 5
ration 15
rational 2
ravenous 8
realm 5
reassure 7
rebellious 12
receptive 11
reciprocal 11
recollect 10
rectify 7
reflect 2
refrain 14
refuge 6
relinquish 14
relish 8
rendezvous 8
renowned 15
repel 16
replenished 10
reprimand 7
repulsive 12
resolution 5
respite 6
restrict 15
revelation 14
revenue 5
reverberate 15

reverie 10
ruse 9

S

saga 4
sanctuary 6
satire 4
saunter 8
scurry 8
secede 19
shrewd 18
sinister 17
skulk 17
slanderer 12
sluggish 9
smolder 13
snare 17
sneer 12
solace 6
solicit 14
solitary 10
solitude 10
spacious 6
species 3
speculate 2
spontaneous 1
squabble 7
stamina 9
status 11
stealthy 18
stifle 17
stride 8
subdue 16
sublime 15
subversive 17
succumb 7
suppress 17
susceptible 1
swagger 12

T

tangible 4
tantalizing 18
temperate 16
tepid 3

terminate 14
thoughtful 10
thrive 10
tolerant 7
toxic 3
trait 3
transcend 1
transformed 10
transition 10
treacherous 17
tremulous 1
trifle 9
truce 16
trying 11
tumult 15
turbulent 11
tyranny 5

U

ultimate 15
uncouth 12
ungainly 9
unique 6
unkempt 6
unruffled 10
unruly 12
unscrupulous 12
unseemly 12

V

valiant 16
vanquish 16
variable 4
velocity 3
venture 10
verify 3
versatile 9
vertical 4
vigilant 16
vigorous 9
vile 18
vindicate 14
vital 15
vulnerable 16

W

waver 9
whet 8
wily 18
wistful 13
woe 6
wrath 13
wretched 13

X–Y

yearn 2

Z

zany 11

Notes

Answer Key

Notes

 ··· *POWer Words™ Grades 7–8*

p. 10
1. c
2. a
3. b
4. a
5. b
6. c
7. a
8. c
9. b
10. a
11. b
12. a
13. b
14. c
15. a
16. b

p. 11
1. c
2. n
3. d
4. h
5. k
6. g
7. l
8. p
9. i
10. e
11. t
12. o
13. r
14. f
15. q
16. b
17. j
18. s
19. m
20. a

p. 12
1. flustered
2. oblivious
3. anticipate
4. genial
5. accommodate
6. peculiar
7. competent
8. motivated
9. tremulous

10. dogged
11. boisterous
12. jovial
13. eloquent
14. Buoyant
15. susceptible
16. inhibited
17. mettle
18. keen
19. assimilate
20. assert
21. transcend
22. mingle
23. elated

p. 14

p. 15
1. garbled
2. monotonous
3. cliché
4. irrelevant
5. illegible
6. humdrum
7. illiterate
8. pondered
9. incomprehensible
10. indefinite
11. rational; ramble
12. perceived
13. grapple
14. cram
15. inquisitive

p. 16
1. cliché
2. cope
3. humdrum
4. speculate
5. incoherent
6. reflect

7. rambling
8. query

Hidden Message: "He was electri-fried."

p. 18
1. hypothesis
2. predict
3. verify
4. astronomy
5. friction
6. orbited
7. velocity
8. palpable
9. fusion
10. traits
11. tepid
12. evolved
13. porous
14. analyzed
15. gravity
16. organism

p. 19
1. r
2. c
3. h
4. l
5. d
6. e
7. k
8. o
9. s
10. a
11. g
12. b
13. f
14. m
15. i
16. t
17. p
18. j
19. q
20. n

p. 20
1. palpable
2. gravity
3. evolved

4. celestial
5. analyzed
6. arid
7. inert
8. toxic
9. porous
10. organisms
11. orbit
12. velocity
13. friction
14. eclipsed
15. species

p. 22

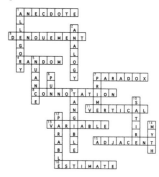

p. 23
1. c
2. c
3. b
4. b
5. c
6. a
7. b
8. c
9. c
10. a
11. b
12. c
13. c
14. a
15. b
16. b

p. 24

1. anecdote
2. connotation
3. literal
4. saga
5. satire
6. approximate
7. infinite
8. pseudonym
9. pun
10. nuance
11. paradox

p. 26

1. c
2. k
3. n
4. a
5. f
6. h
7. b
8. q
9. l
10. g
11. t
12. o
13. j
14. d
15. s
16. m
17. p
18. r
19. e
20. i

p. 27

1. Incentive
2. Apprentices
3. Agenda
4. Diversity
5. Anarchy

6. Boycott
7. Expenditures
8. Revenue

p. 28

1. defect
2. entrepreneurial
3. incentive
4. allegiance
5. amended
6. decreed
7. legacy
8. nomads
9. ratify
10. realms
11. diversity
12. revenue
13. embargo
14. resolution
15. consolidate

p. 29

1. No
2. Yes
3. Yes
4. Yes
5. Yes
6. No
7. Yes
8. No
9. Yes
10. Yes
11. No
12. Yes
13. No
14. No
15. No
16. Yes
17. No
18. Yes
19. No
20. Yes

p. 30

1. decree
2. satire
3. incentive
4. grapple
5. rational
6. .predict

7. adjacent
8. infinite
9. analogy
10. embargo
11. spontaneous
12. analyze
13. toxic
14. yearn
15. genial
16. jovial
17. illegible
18. verify
19. mettle

Hidden Message: "Create An Amazing Life."

p. 31

1. u
2. t
3. f
4. o
5. d
6. a
7. r
8. p
9. g
10. m
11. q
12. l
13. c
14. k
15. b
16. i
17. h
18. s
19. n
20. e

p. 32

1. species
2. velocity
3. inquisitive
4. predicted
5. connotation
6. denouement
7. phenomenon
8. traits
9. abdication
10. resolution

11. immigrants
12. consolidation
13. speculate
14. indefinitely
15. rambling
16. celestial

p. 33

1. anticipate
2. eloquent
3. tremulous
4. susceptible
5. estimate
6. embargo
7. organism
8. myth
9. hypothesis
10. speculate
11. entrepreneur
12. rambling
13. garbled
14. diversity
15. yearn
16. nuance

p. 34

p. 36

1. a
2. c
3. a
4. a
5. b
6. c
7. b
8. b
9. b
10. b
11. a
12. c
13. c

14. b
15. b
16. a

p. 37
1. e
2. a
3. b
4. d
5. c

p. 38
1. respite
2. drab
3. plight
4. unique
5. solace
6. folly
7. affirmation
8. spacious
9. labyrinth
10. immaculate
11. asylum
12. jumble

p. 40

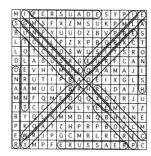

1. probe
2. bellow
3. clamor
4. extraordinary
5. tolerant
6. succumb
7. implore
8. reassure
9. reprimand
10. astonish
11. quibble
12. exhausting
13. impose
14. persuade

p. 41
1. Yes
2. No
3. Yes
4. No
5. Yes
6. Yes
7. No
8. Yes
9. Yes
10. No
11. No
12. Yes
13. Yes
14. No
15. Yes

p. 42
1. instilled *or* fostered
2. implored
3. imposed
4. fostered *or* instilled
5. persuade
6. reassured; extraordinary
7. reprimanded
8. astonished
9. bellow
10. clamor
11. divulge
12. concurs
13. exasperating; squabbling
14. probing
15. abrupt

p. 43
1. folly
2. unique
3. assent
4. asylum
5. succumb
6. drab
7. refuge
8. chaos
9. frank
10. tolerant
11. immaculate
12. marvel
13. woe

14. concur
15. adequate
16. solace
17. quibble
18. unkempt
19. divulge
20. instill
21. labyrinth
22. spacious

p. 44
1. c
2. e
3. d
4. d
5. b
6. a
7. e
8. c

p. 46
1. bestow
2. haggle
3. absurd
4. acquire
5. saunter
6. frivolous
7. lustrous
8. gratify
9. amble
10. rendezvous
11. relish
12. scurry

Hidden Message: "He was a dictator."

p. 47
1. c
2. a
3. b
4. b
5. c
6. b
7. c
8. c
9. b
10. b
11. b
12. c

13. c
14. a
15. c
16. a

p. 48

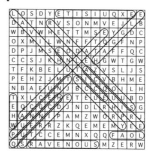

1. acquire
2. rendezvous
3. loaf
4. scurry
5. stride
6. exquisite
7. lavish
8. pungent
9. ravenous
10. whet
11. haggle
12. quench
13. accumulate
14. entice

p. 50
1. fervent
2. forfeit; blunder
3. vigorous
4. flourish
5. prevail; stamina
6. versatile
7. precise; botched
8. inept
9. maneuver
10. feint
11. ruse
12. nimble
13. haphazard
14. painstaking; intricate

p. 51
1. dexterity
2. flourished
3. intricate
4. ruse
5. blunder
6. forfeited
7. frenzied
8. botched
9. sluggish
10. trifle
11. ungainly
12. waver

p. 52
precise
dexterous
nimble
lithe
trifle
inept
waver
versatile
fervent
frenzied

p. 54

p. 55
1. o
2. m
3. k
4. a
5. q
6. u
7. t
8. c
9. f
10. j
11. n
12. d
13. e
14. b
15. i
16. g
17. h
18. l
19. x
20. p
21. v
22. r
23. w
24. s

p. 56
1. transition
2. unruffled
3. solitude
4. venture
5. optimist
6. recollect
7. commence
8. bolster
9. thrive

Hidden Message: "Thanks for that nimble maneuver."

p. 57
1. N; e
2. T; b
3. E; r
4. A; t
5. B; h
6. G; g
7. C; l
8. I; a
9. J; c
10. S; o
11. Q; j
12. M; m
13. D; s
14. K; d
15. L; f
16. F; q
17. O; k
18. H; n
19. R; p
20. P; i

pp. 58–59
1. lustrous
2. frenzied
3. trifle
4. optimist
5. reverie
6. gratify
7. thrive
8. stride
9. stamina
10. forfeit
11. muse
12. amble
13. whet
14. lithe
15. fervent
16. quench
17. exhilaration
18. feint
19. haggle
20. precise
21. replenished
22. absurd
23. jar
24. scurry
25. venture
26. loaf

p. 60
1. d
2. b
3. d
4. e
5. e
6. c
7. c
8. e

p. 61
1. delectable
2. ponder
3. allegiance
4. stamina
5. maze
6. arid
7. invincible
8. flourish
9. waver
10. spacious
11. susceptible
12. realm
13. endeavor
14. inquisitive
15. saga

p. 62
1. b
2. g
3. f
4. h
5. j
6. c
7. n
8. a
9. e
10. l
11. o
12. t
13. i
14. q
15. m
16. r
17. x
18. p
19. w
20. s
21. d
22. v
23. u
24. k

p. 63
1. b
2. c
3. b
4. c
5. c
6. b
7. b
8. a
9. c
10. a
11. b
12. c
13. a
14. c
15. a
16. c

p. 64
1. q
2. h
3. m
4. e
5. s
6. o
7. p
8. t
9. f
10. c
11. k
12. i
13. n
14. j
15. d
16. a
17. l
18. r
19. b
20. g

p. 66
1. accord
2. proximity
3. compassion
4. discretion
5. disposition
6. baffling
7. proficient
8. reciprocal
9. turbulent
10. buffoon
11. fluctuates
12. quirky
13. deprived
14. deluding
15. status
16. forsake

p. 67
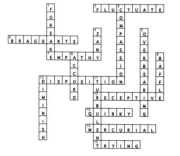

p. 68
1. accord
2. forsake
3. compassionate
4. discretion
5. disposition
6. zany
7. mercurial
8. escalate
9. deprived
10. empathy
11. proficient
12. proximity
13. baffles
14. delude
15. buffoon

p. 70
1. swaggering
2. rebellious
3. impudent
4. lofty
5. gloat
6. hypocrites
7. perjurer's
8. unruly
9. unscrupulous
10. insubordinate
11. blameworthy
12. manipulated
13. unseemly
14. meddler
15. slander

p. 71
1. b
2. e
3. s
4. m
5. c
6. i
7. t
8. r
9. f
10. g
11. n
12. v
13. k
14. u
15. o
16. p
17. j
18. d
19. q
20. h
21. a
22. l

p. 72
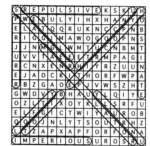

1. bigot
2. swagger
3. imperious
4. uncouth
5. hypocrite
6. lofty
7. obstinate
8. unruly
9. repulsive
10. elite
11. perjurer
12. manipulator

p. 74
1. b
2. b
3. a
4. c
5. c
6. b
7. c
8. b
9. a
10. b
11. a
12. a
13. c
14. a
15. c
16. c

p. 75
1. apprehension
2. deplore
3. forlorn
4. wistful
5. chafe
6. berate
7. cower
8. exuberant
9. wrath

Hidden Message: "They go to see the curator."

p. 76

p. 78
1. terminate
2. avaricious
3. solicit
4. discern
5. impunity
6. divert; aggressively
7. insinuations
8. acknowledged
9. enlightening
10. altercation
11. relinquish
12. vindicate
13. conveyed
14. obliged

p. 79
1. d
2. b
3. j
4. p
5. s
6. l
7. i
8. a

9. r
10. e
11. q
12. f
13. t
14. n
15. h
16. g
17. o
18. c
19. k
20. m

p. 80

1. advice
2. insinuation
3. controversy
4. feud
5. fallacy
6. revelation
7. acknowledge
8. discourse
9. divert
10. terminate
11. discern
12. relinquish

p. 81

1. Yes
2. Yes
3. No
4. No
5. Yes
6. Yes
7. Yes
8. Yes
9. No
10. Yes
11. Yes
12. No
13. No
14. Yes
15. No
16. No
17. No
18. Yes
19. Yes
20. No

p. 82

1. status
2. avarice
3. despair
4. oblige
5. unruly
6. notion
7. buffoon
8. awe
9. wrath
10. discourse
11. lofty
12. proximity
13. curt
14. avid
15. deprive
16. elite

Hidden Message: "Tap Into Who You Are"

p. 83

1. e
2. d
3. e
4. b
5. c
6. e
7. d
8. a

p. 84

1. d
2. c
3. b
4. e
5. c
6. a
7. d
8. e

p. 86

1. crucial; pivotal
2. barrage
3. monitor
4. reverberate
5. confiscate
6. beseeched
7. interminable
8. allotted
9. prevalent
10. prominent *or* renowned
11. compelled; ration
12. restricted
13. novel
14. renowned *or* prominent

p. 87

1. i
2. n
3. b
4. c
5. a
6. t
7. k
8. f
9. q
10. h
11. e
12. m
13. j
14. p
15. d
16. o
17. l
18. g

p. 88

1. prevalent
2. interminable
3. crucial
4. dissuade
5. pinnacle
6. novel
7. alter
8. allot
9. reverberate
10. barrage
11. tumult
12. beseech

13. monitor
14. restrict
15. ultimate
16. pivotal

p. 90

1. b
2. a
3. c
4. c
5. c
6. a
7. a
8. c
9. c
10. b
11. a
12. c
13. c
14. a
15. b
16. c

p. 91

1. No
2. No
3. No
4. Yes
5. Yes
6. No
7. Yes
8. Yes
9. No
10. Yes
11. No
12. Yes
13. No
14. Yes
15. Yes

p. 92

1. eradicate
2. avert
3. valiant; quest
4. confronting
5. foil
6. alliance
7. vigilant
8. just
9. abstain
10. endure

11. quell; ideal
12. forthright
13. intervene
14. empowered

p. 94

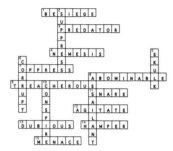

p. 95

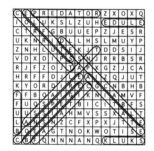

1. fanatic
2. predator
3. assailant
4. sinister
5. treacherous
6. bluff
7. besiege
8. agitate
9. elude
10. skulk
11. conspire
12. corrupt
13. stifle
14. despicable

p. 96

1. c
2. b
3. a
4. b
5. b
6. a
7. c
8. c
9. b

10. a
11. c
12. b
13. a
14. c
15. a
16. b

p. 98

1. bleak; desolate; eerie
2. conjured; hideous; grotesque
3. stealthy
4. vile; putrid
5. murky; tantalizing
6. cunning; wily
7. massive
8. mimicked
9. ominous
10. bewildered
11. shrewd
12. distort

p. 99

1. bewilder
2. distort
3. feign
4. shrewd
5. vile
6. stealthy
7. cunning

Hidden Message: "A Wily Deceiver"

p. 100

1. e
2. j
3. i
4. s
5. h
6. o
7. l
8. q
9. b
10. d
11. t
12. n
13. m
14. a

15. g
16. r
17. p
18. c
19. f
20. k

p. 101

1. D; i
2. I; a
3. M; m
4. A; d
5. S; k
6. P; p
7. B; g
8. F; t
9. G; o
10. K; s
11. N; e
12. J; h
13. C; q
14. E; l
15. H; f
16. L; j
17. Q; r
18. R; c
19. T; n
20. O; b

p. 102
My Hero
Who or What He Is

1. pivotal
2. temperate
3. crucial
4. compelling
5. forthright

His Goal

1. quest
2. alliance

How He'll Get It

1. empower
2. foil
3. dissuade
4. intervene
5. beseech

The Nasty Villain
Who or What He Is

1. fanatical
2. adversarial
3. irksome
4. predator
5. despicable

His Goal

1. agitate
2. corrupt

How He'll Get It

1. deceive
2. bluff
3. oppress
4. conspire
5. alter

p. 103

1. stifle
2. interminable
3. endure
4. abominable
5. dubious
6. enchanted
7. prevalent
8. conspire
9. subversive
10. bleak

p. 104

1. vital
2. renowned
3. beseech
4. compel
5. ration
6. pact
7. integrity
8. alliance
9. predator
10. stifle
11. skulk
12. cunning
13. murky
14. feign
15. wily
16. colossal
17. quell
18. prominent

p. 106
1. c
2. c
3. c
4. c
5. b
6. c
7. a
8. b
9. c
10. a
11. a
12. b
13. b
14. a
15. a
16. c

p. 107
1. idle
2. persecuted; principles
3. punctilious
4. hordes
5. momentum
6. idol
7. prosecuted
8. principal
9. punctuality
10. hoard
11. affect
12. momentous
13. excessive
14. allusion
15. ceded

p. 108

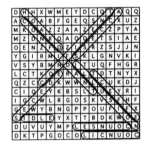

1. access
2. effect
3. illusion
4. secede
5. confidant

6. council
7. counsel
8. confident
9. hoard
10. idle

p. 110
1. accepted
2. adapt
3. complement
4. discreet
5. inflammable
6. compliments
7. flouted
8. except
9. infer
10. abetted
11. incredible
12. hurtled
13. prior

p. 111
1. v
2. t
3. n
4. x
5. w
6. d
7. j
8. l
9. u
10. q
11. p
12. m
13. s
14. b
15. o
16. r
17. c
18. e
19. a
20. h
21. g
22. k
23. i
24. f

p. 112
1. No
2. No
3. No
4. Yes
5. No
6. No
7. Yes
8. No
9. Yes
10. No
11. Yes
12. No
13. Yes
14. No
15. Yes
16. Yes

p. 113
1. idol
2. principle
3. momentous
4. discrete
5. imply
6. punctual
7. infer
8. persecute
9. idle
10. excess

Hidden Message: "He is clueless."

p. 114
1. c
2. a
3. c
4. b
5. c
6. a
7. c
8. c
9. c
10. a
11. c
12. a
13. a
14. b
15. a
16. b

p. 115
1. quirky
2. ethical
3. bleak
4. putrid
5. accord
6. zany
7. massive
8. vile
9. compassion
10. reciprocal
11. slanderer
12. avid
13. barrage
14. avarice
15. intervene
16. bewilder

pp. 116–117
1. escalate
2. gloat
3. awe
4. plague
5. oblige
6. desolate
7. disposition
8. just
9. discreet
10. cringe
11. imply
12. allot
13. principle
14. zany
15. quell
16. aghast
17. idol
18. alter
19. manipulator
20. sneer
21. meddler
22. bluff
23. notion
24. nemesis
25. lofty
26. impunity

p. 118
1. a
2. c
3. a

 ⋯ POWer Words™ Grades 7–8

4. b
5. b
6. a
7. c
8. c
9. a
10. c
11. b
12. b
13. c
14. a
15. a
16. c

p. 119

p. 120

1. imply
2. dubious
3. truce
4. bleak
5. corrupt
6. eerie
7. snare
8. discreet
9. plague
10. monitor
11. endure
12. pivotal
13. adept
14. quest
15. barren
16. irksome
17. hoard
18. counsel

Hidden Message: "You are a 'can do' person."

p. 121

1. menace
2. meddler
3. mercurial
4. mettle
5. amend
6. nemesis
7. momentum
8. momentous
9. blameworthy
10. commence
11. prime
12. perimeter
13. sublime
14. irksome
15. phenomenon
16. complement
17. compliment
18. denouement

p. 122

1. perjurer
2. entrepreneur
3. hypocrite
4. meddlers
5. braggarts
6. immigrant
7. aggressor
8. the valiant
9. fanatics
10. the elite

p. 123

1. l
2. j
3. q
4. o
5. e
6. t
7. g
8. p
9. h
10. f
11. u
12. k
13. c
14. v
15. r
16. b
17. i
18. m
19. d
20. n
21. a
22. s

p. 124

1. c
2. d
3. b
4. a
5. e
6. c
7. d
8. e

Notes